Biggest, Baddest Books

BIGGEST, BADDEST BOOK OF
CAVES

ALEX KUSKOWSKI

Consulting Editor, Diane Craig, M.A./Reading Specialist

Super Sandcastle

An Imprint of Abdo Publishing
www.abdopublishing.com

www.abdopublishing.com

Published by Abdo Publishing, a division of ABDO, PO Box 398166, Minneapolis, Minnesota 55439. Copyright © 2015 by Abdo Consulting Group, Inc. International copyrights reserved in all countries. No part of this book may be reproduced in any form without written permission from the publisher. Super SandCastle™ is a trademark and logo of Abdo Publishing.

Printed in the United States of America, North Mankato, Minnesota
102014
012015

Editor: Liz Salzmann
Content Developer: Nancy Tuminelly
Cover and Interior Design and Production: Colleen Dolphin, Mighty Media, Inc.
Photo Credits: Kenneth Ingham, Shutterstock, Waitomo Glowworm Caves, Wikipedia
(Chris Gray/Rolanddeschain, Piercehendrie, Steinsky, Tod Baker, WTucker, Yerpo)

Library of Congress Cataloging-in-Publication Data

Kuskowski, Alex.
  Biggest, baddest book of caves / Alex Kuskowski.
    pages cm. -- (Biggest, baddest books)
  ISBN 978-1-62403-514-2
  1. Caves--Juvenile literature. I. Title. II. Series: Biggest, baddest books.
  GB601.2.K87 2015
  551.44'7--dc23
                    2014024006

Super SandCastle™ books are created by a team of professional educators, reading specialists, and content developers around five essential components—phonemic awareness, phonics, vocabulary, text comprehension, and fluency—to assist young readers as they develop reading skills and strategies and increase their general knowledge. All books are written, reviewed, and leveled for guided reading, early reading intervention, and Accelerated Reader® programs for use in shared, guided, and independent reading and writing activities to support a balanced approach to literacy instruction.

CONTENTS

CAVES!

Caves are underground spaces.
It can take millions of years to create a cave.

THE SECRET DEEP

Underground caves are hidden in the earth. Scientists study the land looking for clues. Sometimes they find new caves.

SINKING STREAM

Some rivers travel underground. The water may flow into a cave.

SINKHOLES

A cave can form close to the surface. The ground over it is thin. If the ground breaks, it creates a sinkhole.

PITS & SHAFTS

Pits and shafts are holes in the earth. They are vertical caves.

UNDERGROUND DISCOVERY

STONE CHANDELIERS

Water on a cave ceiling dries up. It leaves **minerals** behind. The minerals become rocks called stalactites. They can look like **chandeliers.**

GOOEY CAVE SNOT

Sticky goo called snottite hangs from cave ceilings. Watch out! Snottite has bacteria. It can burn your skin!

BACON STRIPS

Cave bacon is made of mineral-filled rock. The stripes look like bacon. It is so thin you can see light through it!

GROWING ROCKS

Stalagmites grow up from cave floors. Water drips from the ceiling. The drops have **minerals.** The minerals pile up on the floor.

CAVE POPCORN

Cave popcorn is made of water drops filled with minerals. The water splashes on cave walls and floors. The minerals stick together and form bumps.

SUNKEN

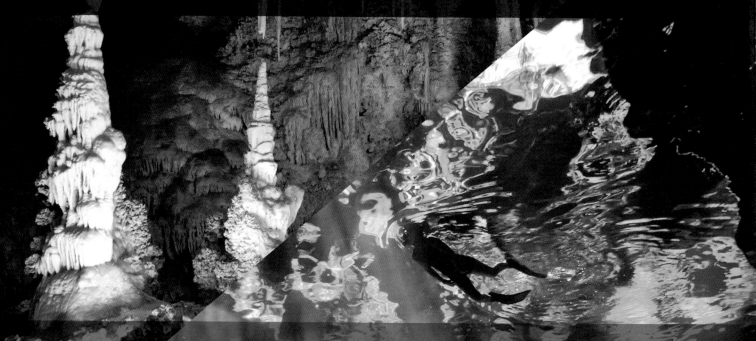

LIMESTONE CAVE

Some places have a lot of limestone underground. Acids in underground water slowly eat away at the limestone. This creates caves. The caves grow over thousands of years.

SEA CAVE

Sea caves are created when waves crash into cliffs. Waves hit the rocks hard. The water washes away the rock.

WORLDS

LAVA CAVE

Lava flows out of **volcanoes**. The top of the lava cools and hardens. The hot lava under it keeps moving. A tunnel is left behind when the hot lava is gone.

ICE CAVE

When giant glaciers melt, the water flows out to sea. Water near the bottom melts first. This makes a cave of ice.

GUIDED BY THE LIGHT

WAITOMO GLOWWORM CAVES

NEW ZEALAND

Look up in the Waitomo Caves. You might think you see stars. But look closer! The "stars" are actually glowworms. The worms make long lines of **mucus**. It hangs from the ceiling. The worms glow to lure insects. The insects fly toward the light. They get trapped in the mucus!

Cave Creatures

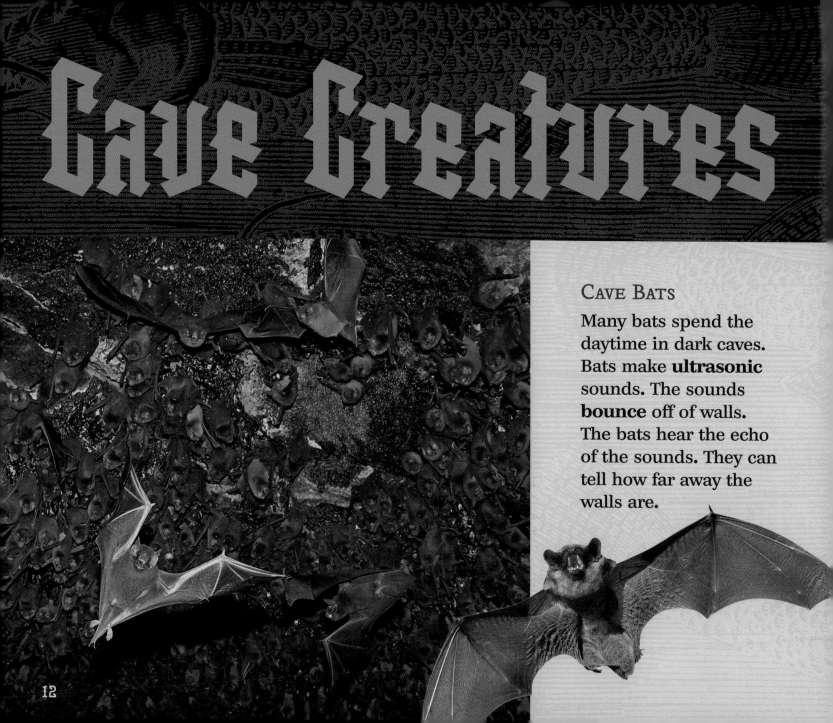

CAVE BATS

Many bats spend the daytime in dark caves. Bats make **ultrasonic** sounds. The sounds **bounce** off of walls. The bats hear the echo of the sounds. They can tell how far away the walls are.

THE HUMAN FISH

The human fish isn't a fish or a human! It is an amphibian. When it finds food, it swallows it whole. But there isn't much food in a cave. The human fish can live for 10 years without food!

BLIND CAVE FISH

Blind cave fish have no eyes and no color. The lack of color helps them hide in the dark. They swim by sensing water pressure.

CREEPY CRAWLY CRITTER CREATURES

FEARLESS CAVE CRICKET

Cave crickets can't see well. But they are fearless. They jump toward predators they can't see to scare them away.

GIANT CENTIPEDE

Amazonian giant centipedes can grow up to 12 inches (30.5 cm) long. They hang by their back legs from cave ceilings. Then they grab bats as they fly past!

CAVE BEETLE

The cave beetle was discovered in 1831. It was the first cave animal to be studied. Before the cave beetle, scientists didn't think anything lived in caves.

EXPLORING THE DARKNESS

GET THE DROP ON CAVING!

Be an underground adventurer. Go caving! Caving is also called spelunking. Cavers explore caves. They make new discoveries. Good cavers know to take along a lot of gear.

Hard Hat
Protect your head from bumps and falling rocks.

Lights
Bring more than one source of light.

Warm Clothes
Caves can be cold. Warm clothing also protects your skin.

Ropes
Ropes help cavers explore steep caves safely.

Boots
Wear boots in caves. They make walking easier. They keep your feet dry too.

The Greatest Cave Explorer Ever Known
Floyd Collins was one of the first people to explore caves in Kentucky. The caves cover hundreds of miles. Collins discovered Crystal Cave in 1917. Today it is part of Mammoth Cave National Park.

eerie Cave echoes

FINGAL'S CAVE

SCOTLAND

Fingal's cave is called "the cave of melody." Wind blows through the cave. It **bounces** off the walls. This creates a constant **eerie** sound.

STONE COLUMNS

Fingal's cave is filled with five-sided columns. Cooling **lava** created them more than 60 million years ago. Many are more than 70 feet (21 m) tall!

THE DEEPEST CAVES IN THE

LONGEST CAVE

MAMMOTH CAVE, U.S.A.

Mammoth Cave is in Kentucky. It has 400 miles (644 km) of tunnels. That makes it the longest cave in the world!

&DARKEST WORLD

DEEPEST CAVE

KRUBERA CAVE, GEORGIA

Krubera is the deepest cave.
It is 7,208 feet (2,197 m) deep.
It is also called Voronya Cave.

BIGGEST CAVE

SON DOONG, VIETNAM

Son Doong is the world's
largest cave tunnel. It is 260
to 490 feet (80 to 150 m)
wide. It is 260 to 660 feet
(80 to 200 m) high. It is
5.6 miles (9 km) long.

HOME SWEET CAVE

ANCIENT HANDS

There are caves in South America and Asia that are covered with handprints.

People pressed their hands to the wall. Then they painted around them.

NATURE'S TOOLS

People made drawings with animal fat and **charcoal.** They painted with fingers, feathers, and sticks.

Caves were humans' first homes. They made cave paintings on the walls. They drew animals and people. The oldest cave paintings were made 40,000 years ago!

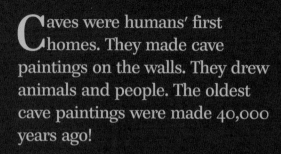

CAVES?

1. STALAGMITES GROW UP FROM CAVE FLOORS. **TRUE OR FALSE?**

2. LIMESTONE CAVES ARE CREATED VERY QUICKLY. **TRUE OR FALSE?**

3. WAITOMO GLOWWORMS GLOW TO LURE INSECTS. **TRUE OR FALSE?**

4. AMAZONIAN GIANT CENTIPEDES CANNOT CATCH BATS. **TRUE OR FALSE?**

ANSWERS: 1) TRUE 2) FALSE 3) TRUE 4) FALSE

23

GLOSSARY

BOUNCE – to spring up or back after hitting something.

CHANDELIER – a fancy light that hangs from the ceiling.

CHARCOAL – the black part of a burned piece of wood.

EERIE – strange and scary.

LAVA – hot, melted rock from inside a volcano.

MINERAL – a naturally occurring, solid substance that is not animal or vegetable, such as metal and some stones.

MUCUS – a slippery, sticky substance produced by the body.

ULTRASONIC – unable to be heard by the human ear.

VOLCANO – a mountain that has lava and ash inside of it.

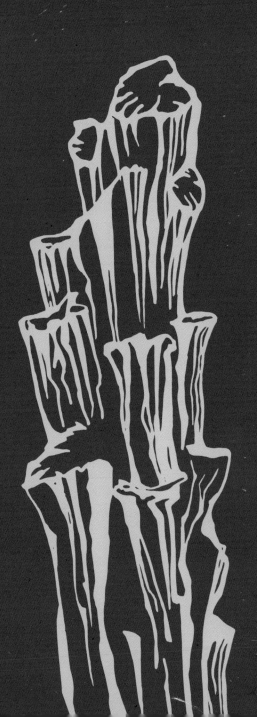

Korean American

Korean
American

Food That Tastes Like Home

Eric Kim

Photographs by Jenny Huang

CLARKSON POTTER/PUBLISHERS

New York

for **Jean**

Contents

Rice Cuisine

Jipbap means "home food" 125

Korea Is a Peninsula

The fish chapter 157

Garden of Jean

The vegetable chapter 179

Feasts

Korean Bakery

The author, shivering, on a boat headed to Niagara Falls in the early 1990s.

Introduction

When I was seventeen years old, I ran away from home. College acceptance letters had just come in, and my mother, Jean, had torn into all of mine before I could come home from school that afternoon. I was so angry with her for opening my mail that I packed a bag in the middle of the night, took the car with the GPS, and drove from our house in Atlanta (where this story begins and ends) to Nashville (where my cousin Semi lived, four hours northwest). In the morning, when Jean saw that my bed was empty and my toothbrush gone, she called me, over and over. In my very first act of rebellion as her son, I didn't pick up.

I remember that trip to Nashville distinctly because Semi and I cooked coq au vin together. By then, as an avid watcher of the Food Network, I had tried my hand at a variety of non-Korean dishes, mostly flash fries and quick pan sauces, but never a proper braise. It was liberating to braise chicken with red wine on Semi's tiny stove, not least because that just wasn't how we cooked back in Georgia. My mother's Korean soups and stews were vociferously boiled, the meat made fall-apart tender in stainless-steel stock pots or burbling earthenware called ttukbaegi. Slow-cooked dishes in general were a whole new frontier for me and wouldn't become a fixture in my home cooking until years later in New York, where I would eventually go to college, take an internship at the Cooking Channel, and buy a yellow Dutch oven with my first paycheck. But for now, at seventeen, tucked away in Semi's Tennessee bachelorette pad, I tasted freedom for the first time in my life. A vast world of pleasures had opened up to me, pleasures that had, until then, been reserved for adults who get to cook whatever they want, however they want, in kitchens that aren't ruled by their parents.

When I came home a few days later, Jean brushed it off, pretended it was a nonissue that I had run away. But she did bring it up at dinner that night: "So, did you have a good trip?" Even then I could tell that she was practicing her loosened grip on me, her second son, the one who never got into trouble. Over a plate of her kimchi fried rice, which she had made for my homecoming (and would continue to make for many homecomings to come), I told her how I had been feeling, paralyzed at that great nexus between childhood and adulthood. I ran away because I needed some space, I explained. Though I didn't say it at the time, she knew what I really meant: I ran away because I needed some space from *her*. This hurt my mother greatly, I could tell. But she smiled and nodded and listened anyway. Seeing that effort—and the hidden worry in her face—was enough to thaw my cold, ungrateful heart. I burst into tears and apologized.

In many ways, I feel that I've been running away from home my whole life. I'm only just now, as an adult, starting to slow down and find my way back to Atlanta, where I was born and raised, to understand its role in my overall story. After a lifetime of running around, I've come to appreciate the stillness of rootedness. It took spending more time, too, in the kitchen as a food writer and journalist, first as an editor for publications like FoodNetwork.com and *Saveur*, and now as a columnist for *The New York Times*, to make me realize that we can never really run away from who we are. Not easily, anyway. This lesson was expounded for me during the Covid-19 pandemic, when I moved back home for one year to work on this cookbook with my mother. I wanted to write down her recipes, but as I got deeper and deeper into the project, I came to the conclusion that my recipes are an evolution of her recipes, and the way I cook now is and will forever be influenced by the way she cooks. This book, then, tells the constantly mutating story of how I have come to understand my identity not just as Jean's son, but also as someone who has always had to straddle two nations: the United States (where I'm from) and South Korea (where my mother is from). Too often I have felt the pangs of this tug of war: Am I Korean or am I American? Only recently have I been able to fully embrace that I am at once both and neither, and something else entirely: I am *Korean American*.

As is often the case with cooking, there are many answers to be found in the kitchen. The recipes in here explore that tension, and the ultimate harmony, between the Korean in me as well as the American in me, through the food my family grew up eating and the food I cook for myself now. At the end of the day, this is all, for me, food that tastes like home, from the Very Good Kimchi Jjigae (page 98) that fuels my weary soul to

Only recently have I been able to fully embrace that I am at once both and neither, and something else entirely: I am *Korean American*.

KOREAN AMERICAN

the Crispy Lemon-Pepper Bulgogi (page 240) that feeds my friends when they come over, or the Gochugaru Shrimp and Roasted-Seaweed Grits (page 40) I make for myself whenever I'm feeling especially homesick for Georgia, and for my mom. This book navigates not only what it means to be Korean American but how, through food and cooking, I was able to find some semblance of strength, acceptance, and confidence to own my own story.

This story is mine to be sure, and my family's. But it's also a story about the Korean American experience, one that in the history of this country is often never at the center. It's about all the beautiful things that come with being different, and all the hard things that come with that, too. My hope is that in reading this book, you'll see yourself in it, whether you're Korean, Korean American, or neither, whether your family immigrated to Atlanta, Los Angeles, or Little Rock. Because at the heart of this book is really a story about what happens when a family bands together to migrate and cross oceans in search of a new home. It's about what happens when, after so much traveling and fighting and hard work, you finally arrive.

There's a pivotal moment that occurs whenever I'm on a long drive home from somewhere distant. The blurry picture starts to come into focus. I can let down my guard and turn off my GPS. The roads are familiar again. I don't need a robot telling me about my own city, my own street, my own hometown. But sometimes, after that long drive, I'll forget to turn off the GPS because my mind is wandering, or maybe I'm listening to a really good song or an especially juicy podcast. And as I roll into my mother's driveway, eager to walk through those doors and crash into my old bed, it'll talk back to me.

"Welcome home."

The Tiger and the Hand

Getting a recipe out of my mother is like pulling teeth out of a tiger's mouth.

It doesn't help that she adds certain ingredients when I'm not looking and accidentally leaves out entire steps when I'm asking her over the phone. Jean (the tiger) doesn't measure anything, so if I (the hand) ever want to replicate one of her dishes, I have to be there in person to watch her make it. This is a common trope in family narratives, to the point where it can sometimes feel rote, clichéd. But it is what it is: Moms need recipe translators, not just for the cooking or for the language, but for the sohn mat, as well.

In Korean cooking, your sohn mat (literally "hand taste") is your bread and butter. It's your signature touch. Sohn mat explains why it can be so hard to replicate your own mother's food, even when you follow her directions word for word, and why yours will never come out exactly like hers (not unlike how a two-finger pinch of salt is different from me to you). So much of a person's sohn mat goes into the food that they cook—their soul, their physicality, and decades upon decades of their personal history. Sohn mat is also a style of cooking. Cooking with sohn mat means cooking by taste, by feel, and by instinct, without measuring cups or spoons. Your sohn mat is considered adept when your food tastes perfectly seasoned and effortless—which comes with experience, but that can also be hard to quantify. It's not just that my mother's generation didn't write down their recipes, it's that their food wasn't cooked with measurements in mind at all. All that knowledge is in the hands and in the heart.

I'd say it's an American impulse to follow written-down recipes to a T. Indeed, it's how many of us learn to cook, through ingredients lists and step-by-step directions on the page (versus the more poetic alternative of standing at your mother's side, learning by watching and memorizing by doing). But so much of my mother's experience involved having to

The author's father, Ki, and his mother, Jean, at a party in Atlanta, Georgia, in the late 1990s.

come up with her own way of doing things. She had to reproduce dishes of her past using new ingredients that were available here in America—like orange sweet potatoes in place of goguma (Korean yellow-fleshed sweet potatoes) or jalapeños in place of kkwarigochu (the Korean word for shishito peppers). Her parents lived thousands of miles away across the Atlantic, so there were few opportunities, save for the expensive long-distance phone call, to casually ask how to cook this or that. And so, the only practical way to cook a motherland dish was to replicate it from taste memory.

Luckily for many, a taste memory can be strong enough to exist as the mental recipe itself. I feel this way about kimchi. The first time I made it on my own in New York, miles away from Jean, I surprised myself at how nearly perfect it came out. This is likely because I grew up not only helping her make it—batches and batches of it at a time—but also helping her taste it throughout the multiday process. No wonder my tongue knew what to look for, years later, when I tackled the project myself. Here's a tip: When in doubt, listen to your tongue. Mine told me when

There will come a day when I can no longer ask my mother how to cook her food. And even the dishes I do know how to cook, I'll have to work out how to make them taste like hers without being able to call her and finesse the details.

to add more fish sauce, more gochugaru, more salted fermented shrimp. And one time, when my kimchi was *way* oversalted, it told me that, too. Like her parents, Jean never wrote down any of her recipes—making me luckier than most, since I can call her to walk me through them. Or I can move back home because of a pandemic and watch her cook them in person. Or, even better, I can help translate those oral recipes to the page and give her food the vocabulary it's never had. Maybe I don't have her *exact* sohn mat, but by quantifying her genius and putting pen to paper, I can at least begin the translation process.

According to the Russian literary critic Viktor Shklovsky, art "exists to make one feel things, to make the stone *stony.*" As a writer, I've always believed that the only way to truly immortalize something is to write it down, make it more permanent. Here's why: There will come a day when I can no longer ask my mother how to cook her food. And even the dishes I do know how to cook, I'll have to work out how to make them taste like hers without being able to call her and finesse the details. Details like: Do you add potatoes to your doenjang jjigae? How much butter goes into your kimchi fried rice? Can you walk me through the ganjang gejang? Again?

Yes. A thumb's worth. And sure, come here, let me show you.

It's something everyone should do. Talk to your parents, your grandparents, your loved ones. Write down their recipes. Don't wait until it's too late.

Fill a large pot with water, soy sauce, and aromatics. Chuck in a sheet of dasima while you're at it. Boil it until it smells like the sea.

How big?

This big. As big as your head.

You'll uncover so much more than food in the process.

The author at his 100-day birthday, making a phone call.

What Is Korean American Cooking?

In 1983, when my parents moved to the United States, there wasn't a single Korean grocery store in their Atlanta suburb. Even the most basic pantry items today—soy sauce, sesame oil, rice vinegar, and certainly gochujang— were either impossible to find or too expensive to buy. They say scarcity breeds innovation. So the story goes that when Korean immigrants moved to Southern California, they couldn't find the cut of short rib meat they ordinarily used for kalbi back home (which was thickly cut along the bone, butterflied, and rolled like a sleeping bag). What they *could* find were flanken-cut ribs (which are thinly cut across the bone, so that each strip of meat has three or four little oblong bones along the top). Not only was this cut cheaper; it was also more readily available at the local Mexican supermarkets. Thus, LA kalbi was born, an exceptionally Korean American dish born of a non-Korean ingredient.

The Korean American food I grew up with has for years been rooted, and arguably stuck, in a particular time and place: 1980s America, the Reagan Era. When my parents came over to the States, they brought with them the version of Korean food that existed then. The YouTube star Maangchi has called this an "immigrant time warp." Korean immigrants were figuring out how to make kimchi in their new kitchens, with the ingredients they could find locally. Some culinary patterns you could pinpoint to the Korean Americanness of our circumstance as immigrants, like the LA kalbi. But what I've come to realize is that there is no clean definition for Korean American food. Every time I've tried to define it, I've failed. There would be exceptions to what felt like patterns. Korean Americanness is, as with any culture, different for every city, every family, every individual. If I were to offer any semblance of codification for this loaded term, Korean American, especially with regard to home cooking, then it'd be this: resourcefulness in the kitchen, using what you have around you, pulling from the past, present, and future to cook what means something to *you* as someone who straddles two nations.

And so, as you use this book, know that when you see a "nontraditional" ingredient in a "traditional" recipe, it's likely because my mother does it that way, not because every single Korean person in the United States does. Or maybe it's the way I do it, or the way my Aunt Julia does it, or the way my Uncle Young did it. Sometimes the reasons we do things in the kitchen can seem arbitrary, but when pressed, there's always a context for our actions. My family, for instance, adores the freshness of jalapeños, which is why so many of these recipes feature them as a star flavoring. Are jalapeños Korean? Not necessarily. But they were the most available at the grocery stores in 1980s Georgia, where my family put down their roots. (We also really love short ribs. And trout fishing. And anything flavored with roasted seaweed.) Anyway, isn't that what food is? Cooking what tastes good to you?

Here's my bottom line: These recipes are Korean American because the people who cook them identify as such. Too often when I publish a family recipe, someone will write to me: "I'm Korean and that's not Korean" (because it doesn't match *their* family's version). But there is more than one way to be Korean. We are infinite. The more we can distance ourselves from this impulse to define entire cultures, cuisines, and experiences as monoliths, the more empathetic we'll become as cooks, and the easier it will be to finally dispel the myth of "authenticity" in food. This requires first and foremost a respect for other people's realities and lived experiences, which are multiple. In this vast, expansive world, this is just one story in the pantheon of Korean American cooking.

For these reasons and more, I encourage you to follow these recipes as they're written. At least the first time. Of course, adapt as you wish after that. This is your kitchen. But if you first follow the recipes as they are written—carefully developed and written by yours truly—then you may learn a thing or two about my family, and maybe even change the way you cook certain things.

I know I did.

Sometimes the reasons we do things in the kitchen can seem arbitrary, but when pressed, there's always a context for our actions. Anyway, isn't that what food is? Cooking what tastes good to you?

Ki and Jean on a mountain, somewhere, in the 1980s.

That Boring Pantry Section in Every Cookbook, but More Fun

I don't know about you, but I always skip the introductory section in cookbooks, the one that walks you through every pantry ingredient as if you've never opened a can of chickpeas in your life. I don't need to tell you how to use a cookbook (or how to open a can), so I won't. But if I'm being realistic, I do know that there may be certain ingredients in here that need explanation, not least because even I didn't cook with some of them before I wrote this book. Many items from the Korean supermarket don't have the English label yet, for instance, which is why I've included the Korean letters here in addition to their Romanizations to help with the shopping.

Jean's pantry is vast and full of secrets. At the start of this book's development, as I sat at the kitchen island watching her cook, she kept wanting to reach for **maesil cheong**, or green plum syrup—to which I said, "No, let's use sugar instead." I thought I was making the recipes more accessible by barring her from her beloved syrup. But more accessible to whom? As we got further into the book process, and as I watched my mother cook in a day-to-day kind of way, I realized what an essential ingredient maesil cheong was to her and how important it was to document the way *she* cooked. Not least because in those details, like this green plum syrup, were magic Korean mom tips.

Maesil cheong doesn't just lend sweetness without the need for sugar, it also adds a slightly tart,

rounded fruitiness that's necessary in certain dishes. I've even started splashing some into hot water in the morning and drinking it as tea. Jean has a homemade bottle of maesil cheong that she only pulls out for special occasions. She calls it "pure medicine" (for its witch-like healing properties). I drink a little whenever my stomach hurts.

Sweetness is important in Korean cuisine because it balances the other flavors—especially all the heat common in many of the kimchis and jjigaes, or stews. People are afraid to use sugar in their savory cooking, but they shouldn't be. It rounds everything out. But where my mother's sweetener is maesil cheong, mine as a recipe developer are **dark brown sugar, maple syrup,** and **honey,** all of which offer something different in flavor and texture. So if I call for one over the other, there's probably a good reason. Oh, and while I'm here: **mirim** is the Korean romanization of mirin.

Let's get another thing straight: In order to use this book, you *need* **gochugaru**—a sweet, fragrant Korean red-pepper powder. Just go out and buy a bag or order one online (it keeps well in the freezer). Not only is it the main ingredient in **kimchi**, it's also a personal favorite pantry item that adds heat, flavor, and nuance to so much of mine and Jean's cooking. Speaking of which, in this book, kimchi gets its own chapter (page 58) because it's something I believe you should cook with, not just eat. And in case this means anything to you, gochugaru is the main ingredient

MAESIL CHEONG (매실청)

SWEETENERS

MIRIM (미림)

GOCHUGARU (고춧가루)

KIMCHI (김치)

GOCHUJANG (고추장)

in **gochujang**, an umami-rich fermented chile paste.

The three jangs in this book (gochujang, doenjang, and ganjang) are very important, what many food publications have called the "Korean mother sauces." But "sauce" is a misnomer here, not to mention that it undersells the pivotal role that jangs play in the repertoire of Korean home cooking. Sometimes they're served as sauces, sometimes they're condiments, but more often than not they *are* the base of the dish, not unlike how a sofrito might underpin a Puerto Rican stew. As the basic building blocks of flavor in my mother's kitchen, the jangs are, like kimchi and gochugaru, essential to Korean food.

DOENJANG (된장)

Doenjang is a fermented soybean paste with great funk and saltiness. You'll see it mostly in stews, or jjigaes, but I love using it as a glaze on fatty fish or as an umami booster in salad dressings. Its byproduct is actually **soup soy sauce**, which is different from regular soy sauce: saltier, richer with glutamates, and lighter in color, all of which means you can add a lot less to flavor a broth or stock without muddying the end result. You probably have the last jang in your pantry already: ganjang, or **soy sauce**. In case it matters to you, we used a Korean brand, Sempio, to develop this cookbook, but you can use whatever you like.

SOUP SOY SAUCE (국간장)

SOY SAUCE (간장)

TOASTED SESAME OIL (참기름)

In these recipes, sesame oil is **toasted sesame oil**, one of the key flavorings in my mother's cooking. A mere drop in anything will trigger in me an involuntary memory.

You'll notice two seaweed products featured heavily throughout the book for their savory properties: **Dasima** is dried kelp, which you can usually find in large plastic bags. One time Jean bought a bag that was bigger than me (!), but even that she broke up into smaller pieces to use easily and regularly throughout the week. Dasima is great for stocks and forms the basis of many of the stews in this book. **Gim** is roasted seaweed that often comes brushed with sesame oil and salt, which is my favorite version—and the one I'm referring to wherever I call for this ingredient. These are also available in large sheets, which are great if you go through as much of it as I do. But most readily available in all grocery stores these days is **roasted seaweed snack,** which is gim that has been cut up into smaller rectangles perfect for popping into your mouth, or for cooking. Where I specify **kimbap gim,** I mean the large sheets that come plain and unseasoned.

DASIMA (다시마)

GIM (김)

KOREAN RADISH (무)

Finally, **Korean radish.** No, not the same thing as daikon radish, and it is not a call for any "Korean-style" radish. It's the cultivar itself, called *Korean radish*. I don't know who named it. Someone should call it something cuter, like cow radish (after its stout, plump shape, which is the main way of telling it apart from all the other radishes I've loved before). It's sweeter and crisper than most radishes and adds an indelibly sweet-bitter roundness to everything.

PANTRY CONTINUES

Aside from these culturally specific ingredients, there are certain pantry items that are used so often in my cooking that they'll be important to know if only to make sure your result comes out like mine.

To get the most controversial bit out of the way: This book was developed using Morton coarse **SALT** **kosher salt,** with the idea in mind that (a) it's so much easier to find across the country than Diamond Crystal, and (b) it's actually saltier than Diamond Crystal by volume, which means there's less chance of you oversalting your food if you do choose to use Diamond Crystal for these recipes. (I'd rather your food need more salt than less of it.)

OLIVE OIL All **olive oil** is regular, not extra-virgin (unless otherwise stated).

EGGS All **eggs** are large and organic. When it comes to eggs, I do try to buy organic, not least because I eat so many of them undercooked, half done, and even raw (the yolk). I'll say what Nigella Lawson once said on the subject of raw eggs: Use ones you feel confident about. There is quite a bit of raw egg yolk action in this book (because it's delicious when stirred into a hot bowl of bibimbap, page 150, or a fiery plate of kimchi fried rice, page 136), and the best thing I can do as a recipe developer is to advise you to use the freshest eggs you can find.

GARLIC All **garlic cloves** are large, and if finely grated, please use a Microplane or other rasp-style grater. I love the way grated garlic melts into food, and it's much easier and faster for me than mincing. But sometimes a mince is needed. If a recipe calls for minced garlic, then Jean's trick for minced garlic is a nice way to go: Using the back of her knife, she sort of crushes them in the first run-through, smashing them up before turning her blade over and mincing through the other way. What you end up with is a mince that's fuzzier at the edges, with less chance of burning. And because there's so much garlic in this book, I recommend buying one of those containers of ready-peeled cloves. (You just bought a Korean American cookbook; you might as well.)

SCALLIONS (파) All **scallions** are large. Use both white and green parts, always. Speaking of scallions, or pa in Korean, you can tell they're important in Korean cuisine because the word for what we call a regular onion is yangpa (or Western onion). Just another example of culture being relative. Beyond pa and yangpa **DAEPA (대파)** is **daepa**, which refers to a much larger scallion that almost looks like a leek (but isn't a leek). Daepa are worth searching for because they provide the umami in so many of the braised soups and stews in this book. You can find them, like most of these ingredients, at the Korean grocery store. They add so much flavor to food that my mom calls them "natural MSG" and prefers using them to regular scallions. Follow Jean's lead and wash, dry, and chop a bunch of daepa into 1-inch pieces, place them in a resealable bag, and freeze them to use whenever you need that extra something-something in your food.

APPLES GINGER Unless stated otherwise, all **red apples** and **ginger** are unpeeled, especially when finely grated or blitzed into a sauce. I never bother to peel either and neither should you (unless you're dying to). As for apple varieties, Jean prefers Fuji—something crisp, sweet but slightly tart, and decidedly not mealy.

RICE

For rice, we eat **medium-grain white rice,** such as Calrose. It has the perfect balance of sticky and fluffy, but you can certainly use whatever type you like best. Note that when I call for cooked white rice (page 128) in a recipe, I mean still-warm, freshly cooked white rice—though with dishes like fried rice, omurice, and bibimbap, where the rice gets reheated for the dish, you could use either fresh, day-old, or even cold.

And though it should go without saying, you may need to shop at a Korean or Asian grocery store for some of the other ingredients, too, like **fresh perilla leaves** (a nuttier, more savory cousin to mint), **fish sauce** (especially Three Crabs brand), **saeujeot** (itty-bitty salted fermented shrimps that come in a jar, for kimchi), **tteok** (those glorious chewy rice cakes), and **Asian probiotic yogurt drinks** (like Maeil Biofeel and Yakult, but especially the former because it's the Korean brand). One thing I'd love for all of us to do is expand our list of local grocery stores. Walking through an H Mart, for instance, will not only open up your worldview and your understanding of other cultures; it'll open up your cooking, too.

PERILLA (깻잎)

**FISH SAUCE
SAEUJEOT
(새우젓)
TTEOK (떡)**

**YOGURT
DRINKS**

And I want that for you. I want that for all of us.

On Serving Sizes

The yields in this book vary depending on each dish's context—culturally, culinarily, and personally. I don't know how much you and your family eat, whether you're feeding small children or hungry prodigal sons. If anything's negotiable in this book, it's the serving sizes of the recipes. Though the cocktails (page 243) and snacks like the dinner toasts (page 33) serve one, they can easily be scaled up. Many of the weeknight meals (pages 31 to 57) serve two to four, and those amounts can be easily doubled, as well. The feasts (pages 210 to 242) serve six to eight, not just because party food is meant to feed people, but because many of those meals taste great as leftovers. Speaking of which, for dishes where leftovers might be optimal, such as the stews (pages 98 to 123), you might see a much larger serving, with the idea in mind that they're often reheated and eaten again throughout the week. That's the joy of a stew.

TV Dinners

Fast foods to eat on the couch

I grew up on food TV. While other kids watched cartoons after school, I parked myself in front of the television to catch the last few hours of primetime Food Network, which introduced me to countless American dishes and cooking techniques I had never seen or tasted before in my mother's Korean kitchen. I found indelible after-school tutors in Emeril Lagasse, Alton Brown, and Rachael Ray, whose *30 Minute Meals* was my introduction to everything from bagged lettuces to seared meats and wine-deglazed pans. Most important, as a kid, I knew that if I wanted to eat this food I was drooling over on the screen, I had to learn to cook it myself.

Like many children of immigrant parents who both worked forty-hour weeks, I was a latchkey kid most weeknights and was, for all intents and purposes, left to fend for myself when it came to dinner. I don't blame them for this. Those pivotal hours between after school and dinnertime taught me self-reliance in the kitchen at an early age. But beyond just teaching me how to cook the American foods I didn't grow up with, Food Network also instilled in me a love for eating in general—which I believe is, in a cyclical way, the key to good home cooking. As Nigella Lawson says most eloquently in her first book, *How to Eat*: "Although it's possible to love eating without being able to cook, I don't believe you can ever really cook unless you love eating."

I use the term "TV dinner" broadly to mean weeknight-friendly fare that's quick to throw together on any given night, but most of all on those evenings when you've just come home after a long day, famished and in need of comfort food. Glass of wine (or whatever) in hand, you can find unlimited solace in taking these dishes to the couch—or straight to bed—to tuck into while catching up on your Netflix queue.

Some of the recipes did indeed come from those latchkey years in front of the television, like the Roasted-Seaweed Avocado Toast (page 34), inspired by the many avocados I ate after school, crushed in a bowl with a shower of crispy, salty gim (roasted seaweed), which also becomes a key ingredient in my pantry pasta (page 39) and creamy grits (page 40). There are plenty of new inventions, too, drawn from that spirit of novelty I felt decades ago as I tinkered in the kitchen and learned to cook for the first time. So while you won't find a recipe for meatloaf and mashed potatoes, you may recognize its key flavors—beef, ketchup, Worcestershire sauce—in my relaxed Meatloaf-Glazed Kalbi with Gamja Salad (page 55). As well, you'll find dishes that count on gochugaru, fish sauce, and toasted sesame oil to lend what are, for me, some of the most nostalgic—and iconic—Korean tastes of my everyday cooking.

Yes, certain meats in this section require marinating, but with a little forethought, you can easily slide them into your weeknight routine. Do it before you go to work in the morning, the night before, or even right as you walk in the door at the end of the day. By the time you've unwound to a Crosby, Stills & Nash record, thirty minutes will have passed and your meat will be beautifully seasoned. All the cuts here cook up pretty quickly anyway, which means you can be on your way to the television in no time—knife, fork, and plate in ravenous hand.

The author (right) and his brother, Kevin (left), playing after school.

Pan-Seared Rib Eye
with Gochujang Butter

Steak night was a big event at our house growing up. Whenever my dad made a significant sale at work, he'd come home with thick, bone-in rib eyes. Destined for the grill, these gorgeously marbled steaks were a cause for celebration because they broke up our usual monotony of stovetop cooking. While my dad tended to the meat on the grill outside, my mom set the table inside with various banchan and the "good" cloth napkins. These were probably the only nights when our dining table wasn't set with bowls of rice, chopsticks, and spoons. Instead, Mom put out forks and steak knives on the table with large white plates to hold the rib eyes (there would still be steamed white rice, of course, just not in bowls). My parents drank red wine with their meal, something they never did with Korean food, while my brother and I had Sprite over ice.

In honor of steak night, when our American dinners would blush Korean edges, it was important to me to have one perfect steak recipe in this book. A bone-in rib eye isn't exactly cheap, so the one thing you don't want to do is mess it up. And my method, in which I season the steak 30 minutes before I plan to cook it, is worthwhile insurance against dryness, as the salt is said to help meat maintain its moisture, even after a hard sear. What's more, this rib eye cooks from start to finish on the stovetop—no oven or grill necessary, which makes things even more manageable. A cast-iron skillet is ideal here, as it conducts heat beautifully and evenly, though any pan would work. The one thing I do highly recommend procuring is an instant-read thermometer; it's yet another way to ensure that the meat reaches your preferred internal temperature of 130° to 135°F for a juicy-pink, medium-rare interior. When it comes to steak, knowledge is power. For those who prefer more of a medium or medium-well, just cook your steaks to a higher internal temperature.

And as much as I respect my father's adoration of A.1. sauce, this steak is finished instead with a hot basting of gochujang butter, an idea I borrowed from a kimchi fried rice recipe in *Koreatown: A Cookbook* by Deuki Hong and Matt Rodbard. It's a magic two-ingredient condiment that works on many things, but especially meat: As you spoon the seasoned butter over the searing steak, the heat from the cast-iron pan causes the sugars in the spicy chile paste to caramelize, leaving behind a sticky, glistening crimson glaze.

RECIPE CONTINUES

1 (1½-pound) bone-in rib-eye steak, about 1½ inches thick

Kosher salt and freshly ground black pepper

3 tablespoons unsalted butter, at room temperature

1 tablespoon gochujang

1 tablespoon vegetable oil

Cooked white rice (page 128), for serving

SERVES 2

Tip If you have time, refrigerate the seasoned steak overnight or for up to 24 hours. Just be sure to let it sit at room temperature for about 30 minutes before cooking.

1. Generously season both sides of the steak with salt and pepper, set on a plate, uncovered, and let it rest at room temperature for 30 minutes.

2. When you're ready to cook, in a small bowl, stir together the butter and gochujang. Set the bowl near the stove.

3. Heat a large cast-iron skillet over medium-high heat. Dab the steak with a paper towel until bone-dry. Drizzle the olive oil over the meat and, using your fingers, smear both sides to coat. Gently place the greased steak into the hot skillet and sear on the first side (without moving it) until a nice golden-brown crust forms, 6 to 8 minutes. Flip and sear on the second side until another golden-brown crust forms, 4 to 6 minutes.

4. At this point, I like to use tongs to stand the steak up, vertically, on its side where the fat cap is (a fat cap is a layer of fat that often borders the edge of a steak—many rib eyes have them; if yours doesn't, don't worry about this step). Hold the steak in place and let it sear until the fat cap gains a golden-brown crust, 1 to 2 minutes.

5. Lay the steak back down on its second side. Immediately add the gochujang butter to the skillet and let it melt and bubble up. Tilt the skillet slightly so the butter pools in one corner, then spoon the hot butter over the steak. Repeat over and over, like you're bathing it, until the internal temperature of the thickest part of the meat reaches 130°F for medium-rare, 1 to 2 minutes. Flip one last time to coat the other side in the gochujang butter. Transfer the steak to a cutting board to rest for at least 10 minutes, or up to 30 minutes.

6. Carve the steak against the grain (that is, perpendicular to the parallel fibers running across the meat); the idea here is that you're shortening those fibers so the meat eats especially tender. On a rib eye, the grain usually runs vertically, which means you have to carve with the knife at an angle to the cutting board to shorten the fibers. Serve with white rice.

Three Dinner Toasts

After school, my brother and I would make elaborate sandwiches with whatever ingredients we could find in the pantry and fridge. It was during these hunger raids that he started adding sugar to his scrambled eggs (which made them taste like gilgeori toast, a Korean street sandwich made with cabbage and sugared eggs), and I crushed roasted seaweed and dribbled a little toasted sesame oil into my avocados (because seaweed and sesame oil taste great on anything). Sometimes it's the simple pairings that work especially well on a slice of toasted white bread. Those taste memories tend to be the sweetest, too, and the most enduring—because you've discovered them on your own.

For those days when you're in a hurry but still want something that feels substantial, these toasts are ideal. You can eat them separately as a snack or together as a meal. You could even make a bunch and serve them as an appetizer, quartered into small squares or triangles. And though I'm calling them dinner toasts, obviously they'd taste great for breakfast or lunch, as well.

Gochujang-Buttered Radish Toast

SERVES 1

1 to 2 large radishes, such as red or watermelon, thinly sliced

1 teaspoon sugar

1 teaspoon rice vinegar

1 tablespoon unsalted butter, at room temperature

1 teaspoon gochujang

1 slice thick, chewy bread, such as country-style sourdough, toasted

Flaky sea salt, for serving

In a small bowl, toss together the radishes, sugar, and vinegar and set aside. In another small bowl, stir together the butter and gochujang until smooth. Spread the gochujang butter over the toast and layer on the quick-pickled radishes, discarding the liquid. Sprinkle flaky sea salt on top (don't skip this step; the salt balances the spicy radishes and the rich butter).

RECIPE CONTINUES

Soft-Scrambled Egg Toast

SERVES 1

2 large eggs

Kosher salt and freshly ground
  black pepper

1 teaspoon sugar

1 tablespoon unsalted butter

1 slice thick, chewy bread, such
  as country-style sourdough,
  toasted

Chopped chives, for garnish

In a small bowl, whisk together the eggs, salt, pepper, and sugar. In a small nonstick skillet, melt the butter over medium-high heat. Add the eggs, stirring constantly with a silicone spatula, just until the eggs begin to curdle and cook through (but are still very runny), 1 to 2 minutes. Mound atop the toasted bread and garnish with chives.

Roasted-Seaweed Avocado Toast

SERVES 1

½ medium avocado, roughly
  cubed

½ (5-gram) packet gim, crushed
  with your hands or snipped
  into thin strips with scissors

1 teaspoon toasted sesame oil

Splash of rice vinegar

Kosher salt and freshly ground
  black pepper

1 slice thick, chewy bread, such
  as country-style sourdough,
  toasted

In a small bowl, gently stir together the avocado, most of the gim, the sesame oil, vinegar, salt, and pepper. Mound atop the toasted bread and top with the reserved gim.

The Quiet Power of Gim

It's not lost on me the fortuitous wonder that my last name is a homonym for gim (often Romanized as kim), or roasted seaweed, one of the greatest Korean pantry items of all time. Everyone thinks of kimchi and gochujang when they think of Korean cooking, but for me nothing tells the story of the peninsular mother country like seaweed, in which South Korea's shores are rich. And gim is, in my book, the purest iteration of this natural resource: paper-thin sheets of dried edible seaweed that have been brushed with toasted sesame oil, sprinkled with salt, and roasted in a pan until crispy. Often cut into smaller rectangular slips, they shatter into a thousand salty pieces as soon as you pop them in your mouth. (And once you pop, the fun don't stop.)

For as long as I can remember, even after we cleared the plates and did the dishes, the one thing that always remained on the dining table was a resealable plastic container of gim, like a savory cookie jar we could reach into once dinner was over and gave way to the longest and most pleasurable portion of the evening: snack time. But the thing is, in Korean cuisine, gim is mostly served as a banchan to be eaten with rice at mealtimes, not just as a snack in between.

One of my earliest memories involves sitting at the breakfast counter in the kitchen, with a bowl of cold white rice and a stack of the onyx-black folios. My mom took the sheets and, using them almost like tissues, grabbed small knucklefuls of rice to create messy, makeshift seaweed rice balls, small enough to shove into my mouth. In Korean, these ugly babies are called jumeokbap ("knuckle rice"), which I've always found endearing. Salty from the gim and comfortingly bland from the rice, knuckle rice was just what my sensitive stomach wanted on early mornings before the school bus arrived.

It was a strange feeling when I started seeing gim in American grocery stores sold as "roasted seaweed snack." Smart marketing ploy, I thought, and not totally inaccurate. (Again, we too ate them like chips growing up.) But what's most quietly magical about gim is that it happens to be an excellent ingredient to *cook* with, a real lesson in minimal effort for maximal effect. You only need a little to make a dish sing. I love the way gim adds a saline hit to anything—and why wouldn't it? All that natural umami is pressed into a single sheet. The sprinkle of salt is important, too, as it distinguishes gim from Japanese nori, which is usually unseasoned. There's also nuttiness, what Koreans call gosoham, thanks to the sesame oil. In fact, many of the recipes you'll see in this book will call for an additional dribble of sesame oil to amplify the nuttiness that's already inherent in gim, because it's that which makes roasted seaweed so irresistible as a flavor profile.

Over the years, tinkering in the kitchen and at various food publications as an editor, I've found that hand-crushed gim is fabulous blended into a salad dressing, stirred into a sour cream dip, and even candied like a brittle. I've used it so much in my recipes that one of my readers once poked fun at me when I posted a cocktail, noting the lack of roasted seaweed in it. (But maybe as a powder mixed with salt, it could make for a lovely rim.) I'm grateful for our current age, and the prevalence of this product on American shelves and online, because it means that I can now call for it in my recipes without worrying about sourcing—or any accusations of narcissism for using an ingredient named after myself.

Creamy Bucatini
with Roasted Seaweed

I present to you what my family calls "gim pasta": a simple, perfect, little black dress of a pantry dish featuring chewy bucatini, roasted seaweed, and cream. These noodles really speak for themselves, in large part because they remind me of the seaside flavors of a classic shrimp Alfredo, but without the meat. This is, perhaps more than any of the other gim dishes in this book, a blatant concretization of my mantra: Roasted seaweed is more than just snack. It's a powerhouse ingredient.

Kosher salt

6 ounces bucatini

1 cup heavy cream

2 large garlic cloves, finely grated

1 tablespoon toasted sesame oil

Freshly ground black pepper and flaky sea salt

20 grams gim, crushed with your hands

Gochugaru (optional), for serving

SERVES 2

1. Bring a large pot of water to a boil and salt it generously. Add the bucatini and cook until pliable, about half the time that the package instructions tell you is al dente. (So if it says cook the pasta for 10 minutes, cook it for 5 minutes.) Reserve 1 cup of the starchy pasta water, then drain the bucatini and return it to the pot.

2. Add the cream, garlic, and about half of the reserved pasta water to the pasta (saving the rest of the water to thin out the sauce later if needed). Bring the sauce to a simmer over medium-high heat, stirring constantly until the sauce reduces by half and slicks the bucatini with garlicky cream, 4 to 5 minutes.

3. Stir in the sesame oil and taste for seasoning. Add more salt if needed (the pasta should be nicely seasoned to bring out the seaweed's natural salinity).

4. Divide the pasta between two plates and finish with freshly ground black pepper, flaky sea salt, and the roasted seaweed snack, showered messily over the bucatini. Dust with gochugaru, if using.

Gochugaru Shrimp
and Roasted-Seaweed Grits

If shrimp and grits were born and raised in the American South by Korean immigrant parents in the early 1990s, then this is what it would taste like. In my version of the Southern classic, the shrimp is first tossed in gochugaru, fish sauce, and *so* much garlic (these ingredients, my mom reminds me, are the start of most recipes for maeuntang, a spicy fish stew, like the one on page 169). The grits are, on the other hand, flavored in the way that a classic Korean jook, or rice porridge, would be flavored: with crushed gim and toasted sesame oil. And when the two combine, it's a beautiful marriage of seaside flavors.

FOR THE GRITS

1 cup whole milk

½ cup quick-cooking grits (not instant)

Kosher salt and freshly ground black pepper

1 tablespoon unsalted butter

2 (5-gram) packets gim, crushed with your hands

2 teaspoons toasted sesame oil

FOR THE SHRIMP

4 large garlic cloves, finely grated

1 tablespoon gochugaru

½ teaspoon celery seed

1 tablespoon toasted sesame oil

Kosher salt and freshly ground black pepper

½ pound jumbo shrimp, peeled and deveined

2 tablespoons unsalted butter

2 teaspoons fish sauce

1 teaspoon fresh lemon juice

Pinch of sugar

Fresh cilantro leaves plus tender stems, for garnish

SERVES 2

1. Cook the grits: In a medium pot, combine 1¼ cups water, the milk, and grits and season with salt and pepper. Bring to a simmer over high heat, then reduce the heat to low. Whisk occasionally and cook until soft and tender, about 10 minutes. The grits should be thick but still loose, meaning they'll coat the back of a spoon and very slowly drip off. (If they're too tight and don't drip in this way, then just add a little more milk.) Add the butter, gim, and sesame oil and stir to combine. Adjust the seasoning with salt and pepper as needed. Keep warm while you prepare the shrimp.

2. Cook the shrimp: In a medium bowl, whisk together the garlic, gochugaru, celery seed, sesame oil, and salt and pepper to taste. Add the shrimp and toss to coat.

3. Set a large skillet over high heat. Melt 1 tablespoon of the butter in the pan. When the butter is hot and the foam begins to subside, add the shrimp in a single layer. Let them cook until lightly browned and no longer opaque (you should see them start to pink up where they hit the pan), 1½ to 2 minutes. Use tongs to turn them over and cook the second side until similarly blushed, about 1 minute more. Remove from the heat and add the fish sauce, lemon juice, sugar, and remaining 1 tablespoon butter. Set over low heat and toss together until the butter has melted and coats the shrimp in a shiny orange-red sauce, and the shrimp are cooked through, 1 to 2 minutes.

4. To serve, spoon the grits onto a large platter or into individual bowls, then top with the saucy shrimp. Garnish liberally with the cilantro.

Maple-Candied Spam

If you grew up Korean, then chances are Spam was one of the first things you learned to cook for yourself. That's because it doesn't take much to slice and pan-sear the beloved Hormel pork product. As an adult, I find myself experimenting with it endlessly, and this is easily my favorite preparation now: roasted in the oven until crispy, then candied in an aromatic pool of maple syrup and garlic powder. The glassy, caramelly exterior adds contrast both in flavor and in texture to the soft, salty dream within. Like most banchan, this tastes best with a bowl of steamed white rice and a few sheets of gim to use as vessels for the pork and rice. Or you could enjoy it as is with an ice-cold beer.

1 (12-ounce) can Spam, sliced ¼ inch thick

¼ cup maple syrup

½ teaspoon garlic powder

Toasted sesame oil

SERVES 4 TO 6

1. On a sheet pan, evenly space out the sliced Spam and place in a cold oven. Turn the oven to 400°F and roast the Spam until lightly browned and crispy, about 25 minutes.

2. Meanwhile, in a small dish, stir together the maple syrup and garlic powder.

3. When the Spam is done, remove the pan from the oven and drizzle the garlicky maple syrup over the Spam. Return the pan to the oven and roast until the maple syrup starts to bubble up and reduce, about 10 more minutes. Watch carefully so it doesn't burn.

4. Lightly grease a large plate with sesame oil. Transfer the Spam to the plate to cool slightly. It will continue to harden as it cools.

Jalapeño-Marinated Chicken Tacos
with Watermelon Muchim

The inspiration for this marinade comes from my Aunt Julia, who immigrated to Uruguay from South Korea in the 1980s. The best thing she ever taught me was how fresh your food can taste if you cook with jalapeños not just as an element of heat in a dish, but as a main ingredient itself. Jalapeños have their own vegetal flavor that can cut through richness beautifully, providing balance. Case in point: This garlicky, chile-packed marinade dyes juicy boneless chicken thighs a glorious bright green color and tastes fabulous inside soft flour tortillas.

To pick up the meaty flavors of the dish, I like to make a spicy relish of fresh watermelon and gochugaru to serve alongside (Jean would call this a muchim, which describes a category of dressed salads and other banchan). Whatever you call it, the cool watermelon tastes fab against the warm, spicy chicken and almost reminds me of tomatoes, but sweeter and juicier. If you're not a fan of heat, then I would seed the jalapeños before blitzing them into the marinade—but if you're like my family, then you'll love this as is.

FOR THE MARINATED CHICKEN

4 large jalapeños, whole (or halved and seeded for less heat)

4 large garlic cloves, peeled

1 cup packed cilantro stems (from 1 large bunch)

½ cup olive oil

2 teaspoons kosher salt

1 teaspoon sugar

1 teaspoon freshly ground black pepper

2 pounds boneless, skinless chicken thighs, cut into 2-inch pieces

FOR THE WATERMELON MUCHIM

1 cup diced watermelon

1 large jalapeño, thinly sliced into rings

1 teaspoon gochugaru

1 teaspoon rice vinegar

¼ teaspoon fish sauce

¼ teaspoon toasted sesame oil

Pinch of sugar

Kosher salt and freshly ground black pepper

FOR THE TACOS

10 to 12 small (6-inch) soft flour tortillas

Cilantro leaves, for serving

Lime wedges, for serving

SERVES 4 TO 6

1. Marinate the chicken: In a food processor or blender, blitz together the jalapeños, garlic, cilantro stems, olive oil, salt, sugar, and black pepper until smooth. Add the marinade to a medium bowl, followed by the chicken, and toss to coat. Set aside to marinate at room temperature for 30 minutes or refrigerate, covered, for up to 8 hours.

2. Preheat the oven to 400°F. Line a sheet pan with parchment paper.

3. Using a slotted spoon or your fingers, remove the chicken pieces from the marinade and transfer to the lined sheet pan. Roast the chicken until it begins to brown at the edges and is cooked through and no longer pink in the middle, 25 to 30 minutes.

4. Meanwhile, make the watermelon muchim: In a small bowl, stir together the watermelon, jalapeño rings, gochugaru, vinegar, fish sauce, sesame oil, sugar, and salt and black pepper to taste and set aside.

5. When you're ready to taco up, heat the tortillas in a dry pan or over a low open flame, turning them often, until warmed through (and slightly charred if warming over a flame). Top each tortilla with a couple pieces of chicken, a spoonful of watermelon muchim, and some cilantro leaves. Serve with the lime wedges.

A Lot of Cabbage with Curried Chicken Cutlets

Donkkasseu (also known as tonkatsu in Japanese) was a regular staple in our house, and undeniably a favorite TV dinner. Since Jean worked, she would bread the pork cutlets ahead of time and store them in the freezer in individual bags. Whenever we wanted to eat them, all we had to do was take them out, thaw them in the microwave, and pan-fry them in a little oil. I'm almost hesitant to say *fry* here because you're really just searing them. Contrary to popular belief, you don't need to deep-fry cutlets for them to get crispy and delicious; you just need a hot pan and a thin layer of fat.

Here I've replaced the pork chops with chicken breasts and added a little curry powder to the breading as an echo of the fabulous combo that is kkasseu and curry. A simple kkasseu sauce comes together in just three ingredients (and tastes way better than bottled). The most important component of this dish is, however, the cabbage slaw, which I've quick-pickled like "chicken mu," those sweet white cubes of Korean radish often served alongside Korean fried chicken. As much as I adore chicken, cabbage will always be, for me, the star.

FOR THE CABBAGE

2 tablespoons rice vinegar

2 tablespoons sugar

½ teaspoon kosher salt

½ pound green cabbage, cored and as thinly sliced as possible (about 3 cups)

FOR THE KKASSEU SAUCE

2 tablespoons Worcestershire sauce

2 tablespoons ketchup

1 tablespoon dark brown sugar

FOR THE CHICKEN CUTLETS

2 boneless, skinless chicken breasts (6 to 8 ounces each)

Kosher salt and freshly ground black pepper

¼ cup mayonnaise

2 tablespoons Dijon mustard

1 cup panko bread crumbs, plus more as needed

1½ teaspoons curry powder

1 teaspoon garlic powder

4 tablespoons vegetable oil

Cooked white rice (page 128), for serving

SERVES 2

1. **Prepare the cabbage:** In a medium bowl, whisk together ¼ cup water, the vinegar, sugar, and salt until the sugar and salt are dissolved. Add the cabbage and toss until well coated. Set aside.

2. **Make the kkasseu sauce:** In a small bowl, stir together the Worcestershire sauce, ketchup, and brown sugar until smooth. Set aside.

RECIPE CONTINUES

3. Make the chicken cutlets: Place the chicken breasts between two sheets of parchment paper or plastic wrap (or in a large resealable plastic bag) and pound them with a rolling pin until they are flat and uniformly ¼-inch thick. Season with salt and pepper on both sides.

4. On a large plate, stir together the mayonnaise and mustard. On another large plate, stir together the panko, curry powder, garlic powder, and some salt and pepper. Set the chicken on the first plate and smother both sides with the mayo-mustard mixture. Then transfer chicken to the second plate and press down, flipping and pressing down multiple times to ensure even panko stickage on both sides.

5. In a large skillet, heat 2 table-spoons of the oil over high heat until hot and shimmering. Add one of the chicken cutlets and fry until golden and crisp, about 2 minutes. Turn the chicken over and fry on the second side until the chicken is cooked through, 1 to 2 minutes. Transfer to a large plate, wipe the skillet out with a paper towel, and repeat with the remaining 2 tablespoons oil and the second cutlet.

6. To serve, divide the cutlets between two plates and pour the kkasseu sauce over each cutlet. Divide the quick-pickled cabbage between the two plates and add some white rice alongside.

Salt-and-Pepper Pork Chops
with Vinegared Scallions

"I think my body likes it when I eat pork," Jean says every time we have pork for dinner. Her affinity for pork—especially the fatty cuts from the ribs, belly, and shoulder—underpins a general theory I have regarding her past life as a tiger (her Korean zodiac sign). But the thing is, my mother never cooked pork chops growing up, which I've always found interesting considering pork features in so much of her daily cooking, and indeed in Korean cuisine.

Years later, in high school, I found that pork chops could be total lifesavers when I needed a quick, lean protein for dinner, not to mention they happened to be surprisingly affordable, especially the thin ones. As I fried them for myself after school, Jean would come home from work and take bites out of any leftovers, which would be sitting on the kitchen counter covered in plastic wrap. Because of this, for Jean, pork chops have always seemed American. Which is funny because to me they taste Korean. When seasoned simply with salt and pepper, they remind me of samgyeopsal, or grilled pork belly, the kind you'd eat at a Korean barbecue restaurant, just from a different life and with less fat (not that there's anything wrong with a little lard).

I love this preparation on thick, bone-in chops, too, as the simple palate lets you taste the pork as it is: rich, meaty, and just a touch gamey (but in the best way). It'll make you go: Oh, *that's* what pork tastes like. For an even cook, these pork chops get pan-fried for a couple minutes per side, then finished in the oven. A simple dipping sauce of sesame oil, salt, pepper, and brown sugar adds a third element, nuttiness, and echoes the samgyeopsal inspiration. The scallions here are a nod to pa muchim, that wonderful gochugaru-slicked scallion salad that often accompanies samgyeopsal to cut the richness of the meat with its sharp allium power.

RECIPE CONTINUES

FOR THE PORK CHOPS

2 teaspoons kosher salt

2 teaspoons freshly ground black pepper

2 teaspoons dark brown sugar

2 bone-in pork chops, 1 inch thick (about 10 ounces each)

2 tablespoons vegetable oil

FOR THE VINEGARED SCALLIONS

4 scallions, cut into 3-inch segments, then thinly sliced lengthwise into strips

1 tablespoon rice vinegar

1 tablespoon gochugaru

Pinch of dark brown sugar

Kosher salt and freshly ground black pepper

TO FINISH

Kosher salt and freshly ground black pepper

Dark brown sugar

2 tablespoons toasted sesame oil

Cooked white rice (page 128), for serving

SERVES 2

1. Prepare the pork chops: In a small bowl, stir together the salt, pepper, and brown sugar. Sprinkle the rub generously on both sides of the pork chops and let them dry-brine at room temperature for 30 minutes or up to 1 hour (any longer and you'll end up with deli meat).

2. Preheat the oven to 400°F.

3. When ready to cook, blot both sides of the pork chops with a paper towel (removing the moisture will help you get a nicely browned crust) and smear the oil on both sides of each pork chop with your hands.

4. Heat a large cast-iron skillet over high heat until very, very hot (you might see a wisp of smoke). Sear the pork chops until nicely browned, 2 minutes on the first side, then repeat on the second side, just 1 minute this time.

5. Transfer the pan to the oven and roast until the internal temperature of the meat reaches 145°F, 8 to 10 minutes

(with a thick pork chop, to get an accurate read, you'll need to use tongs to hold the chop and then carefully insert the thermometer laterally from the side). Remove the pan from the oven and set the pork chops aside on two serving plates to rest while you prepare the scallion salad and dipping sauce.

6. Make the vinegared scallions: In a medium bowl, toss together the scallions, vinegar, gochugaru, and brown sugar. Season generously with salt and pepper and scatter messily over the pork chops.

7. To finish: Make the dipping sauce by adding a pinch each of salt, pepper, and brown sugar to two small dishes. Add 1 tablespoon sesame oil to each dish and stir until the sugar dissolves.

8. Serve each scallion-bedecked pork chop alongside a mound of white rice and the dipping sauce on the side (see Note).

Note For the perfect bite, what I like to do is carve the meat with a fork and knife and drag each piece through the dipping sauce before eating with some of the scallions. Then, for relief, I chase that nutty, salty, sour, and sweet flavor bomb with a bite of white rice.

Cheesy Corn and Ranch Pizza
with Black-Pepper Honey

You *could* make your own pizza dough. (My favorite recipe is Bobby Flay's on FoodNetwork.com; it's simple, straightforward, and tastes great every time.) But more often than not, I like to buy frozen dough or even the kind that comes in a tube, which is perfect for a quick meal. I never apologize for a good shortcut. What does matter are the toppings: One of the greatest revelations I had on a recent trip to the Motherland was the pivotal role that sweetness played in the pizzas there, thanks to ingredients like corn, goguma (Korean sweet potato), and yes, ranch dressing. Ranch lends creaminess but also a dulcet savoriness that's reminiscent of a peppy Alfredo sauce. Additionally, as avid fans of California Pizza Kitchen's barbecue chicken pizza, Jean and I decided to emulate it by adding cilantro and red onion. The jalapeño is a nod to my aunts Julia and Georgia, who both love cooking with the fruity green chiles.

That pizza is great on its own, but the pièce de résistance is the black-pepper honey. At one Italian restaurant my cousin Eunbi took me to in Seoul, they served pizzas with little dishes of runny honey, which, alongside a white pizza like this, turns out to be an excellent dipping sauce for the crust. Just trust me.

2 tablespoons olive oil

1 (10-ounce) ball store-bought or homemade pizza dough

½ cup store-bought ranch dressing

1½ cups shredded low-moisture mozzarella cheese

1 cup fresh corn kernels (from 2 medium ears)

1 cup packed fresh cilantro leaves plus tender stems

1 small red onion, halved and thinly sliced

1 large jalapeño, thinly sliced into rings

Honey (especially the plastic bear kind), for serving

Freshly ground black pepper, for serving

MAKES ONE 9 × 13-INCH PIZZA

1. Preheat the oven to 450°F.

2. Grease a 9 × 13-inch sheet pan with 1 tablespoon olive oil. Place the dough in the pan and use your fingers to push it across the pan and into the corners as best as you can. Spread the ranch dressing evenly over the dough, then sprinkle with the mozzarella. Top with the corn, cilantro, red onion, and jalapeño, and drizzle the vegetables with the remaining tablespoon of olive oil.

3. Bake until the crust is browned and the toppings are slightly caramelized, 20 to 25 minutes.

4. Cool for at least 10 minutes before cutting into squares. Pour the honey into a small dish, add a few pinches of the pepper, and serve alongside the pizza.

Meatloaf-Glazed Kalbi
with Gamja Salad

When I was a kid, I adored TV dinners—you know, the frozen kind that came on a tray, sometimes with a dessert included if you were lucky. My favorite was the meatloaf with mashed potatoes, not least because it was so far from anything my mother ever cooked for us. It felt like a stolen treat. The meatloaf was salty but sweet like candy, topped with the most noble of condiments (ketchup), and the potatoes were always dry at the edges (not in a bad way or anything; in fact, I was quite fond of the way they microwaved into a crispy-chewy mass that you could lift out in one piece). As I got older, I certainly ate fewer of these frozen meals, though my nostalgia for them remained, albeit in more grown-up ways: like in these flanken-cut beef short ribs (or LA-style kalbi), which get crispily burnished in a pan and lacquered in a sticky, saucy glaze of garlic, ketchup, Worcestershire sauce, and brown sugar. I call these ribs "meatloaf-glazed" because their flavor profile reminds me of those ketchup-laden frozen meatloaves I ate for all those years in front of the television after school watching Food Network.

But if you were to ask my mother, this dish, especially alongside the gamja (potato) salad, reminds *her* of the American-style restaurants she frequented during her college days in Seoul, back in the early 1980s, when her hair was as big as her hoop earrings. As she tells it, these gyungyangsik (Western cuisine) restaurants were peak *cool*. They played American pop songs and served Westernized dishes like omurice (ketchupy fried rice with an omelet), donkkasseu (fried, crunchy pork cutlets), and hambak steak (a ground beef entree reminiscent of Salisbury steak). There's a flavor thread in all these dishes: ketchup and Worcestershire sauce. Jean, a newly minted freshman in college, would go to those hip restaurants to meet friends, or on dates. Back then, she says, you weren't allowed to go there as a kid or even as a high schooler; they were for grown-ups. (I smiled thinking of how "old" she must've been when she went to these restaurants for the first time on her own: eighteen, maybe nineteen.)

RECIPE CONTINUES

Perhaps what I love most about this recipe in particular, aside from the fact that my mother and I developed it together, is that it reminds both of us of our pasts, albeit different decades and different countries. It makes me wonder why certain flavors like ketchup and Worcestershire sauce are so stuck in time, never updated or brought into the present, where we exist now as adults. I suppose their nostalgia value is largely what makes them taste so good, because food is always more than just fuel. Taste memories span time and space. Like the best "TV dinners," this one doesn't require much of you at all. You do have to boil some potatoes for the salad. They get mashed with hard-boiled eggs and mayo and studded with various vegetables: cucumbers for crunch, and carrots, corn, and peas for sweetness and color. My mom always kept a bag of that vegetable mix in our freezer, which is why, to this day, whenever I see the colors orange, yellow, and green, I'm flooded with memories of that frozen garden of hers. Sure, you could dice your own fresh carrots and shuck your own corn. But in this case, why bother?

FOR THE GAMJA SALAD

1 medium cucumber, diced

Kosher salt

2 pounds russet potatoes (2 to 3), peeled and cut into 2-inch chunks

2 large eggs

½ cup frozen diced carrots

½ cup frozen corn kernels

½ cup frozen peas

¾ cup mayonnaise

2 teaspoons rice vinegar

1 teaspoon sugar

Freshly ground black pepper

FOR THE KALBI

½ cup ketchup

4 large garlic cloves, finely grated

2 tablespoons dark brown sugar

1 tablespoon Worcestershire sauce

1 teaspoon rice vinegar

1 teaspoon dried oregano

Kosher salt and freshly ground black pepper

2 pounds flanken-cut beef short ribs (LA-style kalbi), about ¼ inch thick

1 tablespoon vegetable oil

SERVES 4

1. Make the gamja salad: In a small bowl, toss together the cucumber and 1 teaspoon salt and set aside.

2. Bring a large pot of water to a boil and salt generously. Add the potatoes and eggs and cook the eggs for 10 minutes and the potatoes until fork-tender, 15 to 20 minutes. While the potatoes continue to cook, run the hard-boiled eggs under cold tap water to cool, then peel. Chop up the peeled eggs as finely as you can.

3. Drain the potatoes and return them to the pot along with the chopped eggs, then mash with a fork, a whisk, or a potato masher. Add the frozen vegetables to the hot potatoes (so they can thaw) and stir. Fold in the salted cucumbers (leaving behind any liquid). Add the mayonnaise, vinegar, and sugar, and season with salt and pepper. Set the potatoes aside, covered, while you cook the short ribs.

4. Make the kalbi: In a small bowl, stir together the ketchup, garlic, brown sugar, Worcestershire sauce, rice vinegar, oregano, and ½ teaspoon salt. Season with pepper and set the sauce aside.

5. Rinse the short ribs under cold tap water to get rid of any bone fragments. Pat them dry and then season with salt and pepper on both sides. Heat a large skillet over medium-high heat and add the vegetable oil.

Place half of the short ribs in a single layer, without crowding the pan, and sear both sides until deeply browned and almost charred at the edges, about 8 minutes total. Remove the ribs from the pan. Repeat with the rest of the meat. When the second batch is done cooking, return the first batch of ribs to the pan and turn off the heat.

6. Add the sauce to the pan and toss the ribs until evenly sticky and well coated, letting the residual heat reduce the sauce slightly, 1 to 2 minutes.

7. Transfer the ribs to a platter and serve alongside a scoop or two of the potato salad, which can be eaten cold or at room temperature.

The author and his mother, Jean, many years ago.

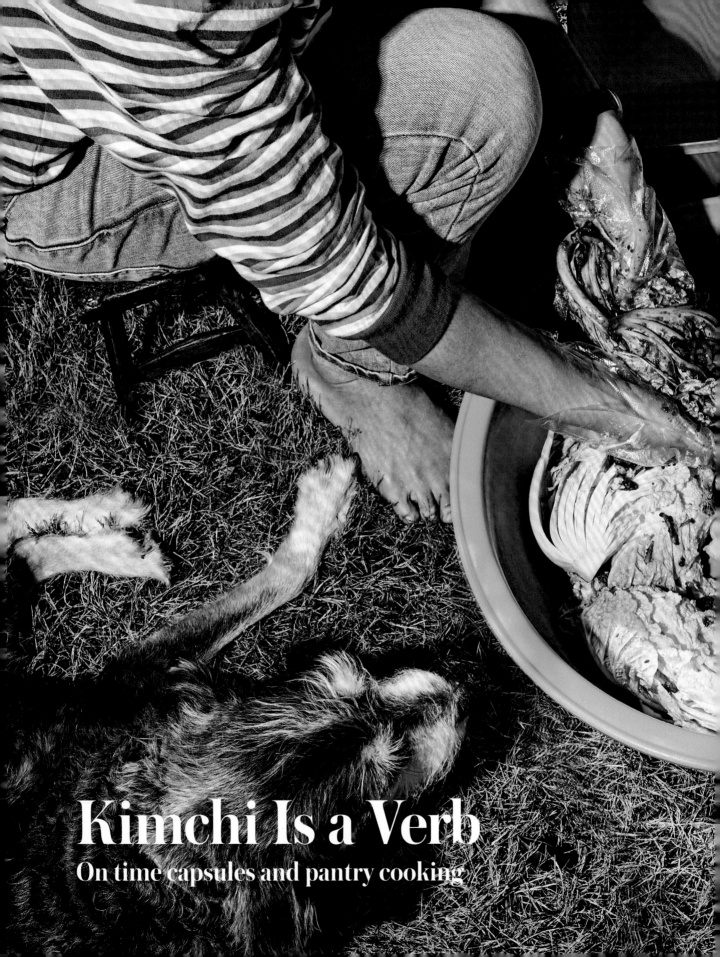

Kimchi Is a Verb
On time capsules and pantry cooking

Let me start off by saying that, no, kimchi is not literally a verb. It's a noun used to describe an array of salted vegetables fermented until sour with lactic acid bacteria. And while a jar of the red, cabbage-based variety is probably sitting in your fridge right now—and is, to be sure, a mainstay of Korean cuisine—there are a million other shapes, sizes, and flavors in the pantheon of kimchis. "Many things, like cucumbers, chives, and apples, can also be kimchi'd," write Deuki Hong and Matt Rodbard in *Koreatown: A Cookbook,* in which they explore the myriad ways in which kimchi is more of a technique than just a single item, "more of a verb than a noun."

The redness comes from gochugaru, by the way, and not all kimchis have it. Take, for instance, my mother's Baek Kimchi with Beet (page 70). Baek (white) kimchi is normally a refreshing napa cabbage kimchi sans gochugaru, hence the distinction of its color. But in this case, it's dyed magenta from beets, which lend a deep and dreamy earthiness in addition to that electric color. Without the spice, you can really taste the cabbage's natural sweetness. I love dishes like this that accentuate a food's inherent goodness (sort of like a good editor). Take out the beets, and that baek kimchi is actually a closer approximation to what kimchi-ing was all about in ancient Korea. (Red chile peppers didn't arrive on the Korean Peninsula until the late sixteenth century.)

Eventually, maybe, you'll start to make your own kimchi at home (try Jean's treasured recipe, page 68). And hopefully, you'll find that the whole rigamarole is really not as complicated as everyone makes it out to be, and can even be a lot of fun when done with friends. Even more, you'll discover that there's a vast world of alternative roots, grasses, and vegetables out there to kimchi. My mother is the master of verbing kimchi, which is why we can thank her for most of the recipes in this chapter. Her mantra has always been, "When in doubt, kimchi it." If only everything in life were that easy. But she does have a point: Kimchi-ing is just one of many ways in which you can preserve the past and have it with you forever, or at least for as long as the supply lasts. It's also a great way to use up produce before it goes bad, and before you know what to do with it.

My main point is that you can incorporate kimchi into your life in whatever capacity works for you—and not just as a method for preserving vegetables and eating them straight out of the jar like a pickle, but using them as an ingredient to *cook* with, as well (which is what the recipes in the second half of this chapter are dedicated to). A gorgeous, well-fermented baechu, or napa cabbage, kimchi can be an instant way to transform any dish with the flick of a wooden spoon, like the Caramelized-Kimchi Baked Potatoes (page 91) or the Bacon-Fat Kimchi Jeon with Herbs (page 88). By cooking kimchi in a pan, you can caramelize its sugars, completely transforming its sharp funkiness into a deep and mellow savoriness.

Kimchi, as a concept more than a definitive thing, is the bedrock of Korean cuisine and a staple of the Korean pantry. Even as an American, I can say with confidence that kimchi is at the soul of my Koreanness, from its sharp taste to the metaphor born of its preservation and survival through the harshest of winters. There's great comfort in knowing that, from a single jar of kimchi, you can have meals for months to come. As long as there's kimchi in the house, there's always something to eat.

Kimchi Is a Time Capsule

Jean's kimchi fridges (plural) are a testament to this concept that you can kimchi just about anything. Sorting through her stash among the multiple fridges is like digging for buried treasure. Sometimes, when I'm feeling really greedy, I'll pull out as many different jars of kimchi as I can from Jean's stockpile (my favorites are the bitterer ones like gat, or mustard green, kimchi; burdock kimchi, which tastes like a more muted but complex ginger; and garlic scape kimchi, which has excellent crunch). After enjoying a simple meal of white rice and all of these kimchis, maybe with a fried egg or a stew, I'll fail miserably at trying to put the jars back so they fit. It's like a game of Tetris, one I always lose.

"I'll do it, I'll do it." Jean often has to take over and rearrange a few things to make sure all her kimchis can fit. And they *must* fit: They're stored here at that perfect kimchi-fridge temperature (a degree above freezing), which prevents the stash from fermenting too quickly. Recently she started putting Post-it notes on the different jars so it'd be easier to know which ones to pull out. In the Before Times (that is, before the Post-it notes), we used to have to open each lid to see what was inside. Now we can just read her labels.

I love peering into these fridges. They're time capsules: Some jars I've made with her and others she's inherited from her sisters in Korea. The fridge is especially full in the fall, during kimjang season. A kimjang is an annual kimchi-making event, usually done communally, to preserve the late-summer and fall cabbage crop through the winter season (not unlike a tamalada or a dumpling-making party, but for kimchi). One kimjang's worth of kimchi—often pounds and pounds of the stuff—is meant to last you for a year. Though it's true that making kimchi is much easier with two sets of hands or more, there is something to be said about the calm and quiet of a solo kimjang. I sometimes prefer making kimchi alone because it takes time, and I want to fill that time with podcasts, music, ASMR videos, and other "me" things that make me happy. Not to mention the jar of kimchi itself is, for me, the supremest act of kindness to my future self, an example of what I like to call time-capsule cooking (the kind of make-ahead food that you don't get to cash in on until later). When it comes to fermentation, it's the wait that makes the end reward taste especially sweet.

Jean kimjangs alone, too. When asked how often she makes kimchi alone, she said: multiple times a month. Our family *does* go through a lot of kimchi, but I think the point isn't that we eat this much kimchi, but that she never wants to be without it. Even growing up, when we traveled as a family, my mother would freeze kimchi sauce in little plastic bags and bring it wherever we went. For fear of living just one week without kimchi, she would fly with this sauce so that she could dress whatever produce was native to wherever we were visiting. For Jean, kimchi should never be more than a frozen bag of sauce away—further proof that it's a gift that spans temporality, an act of kindness for future you.

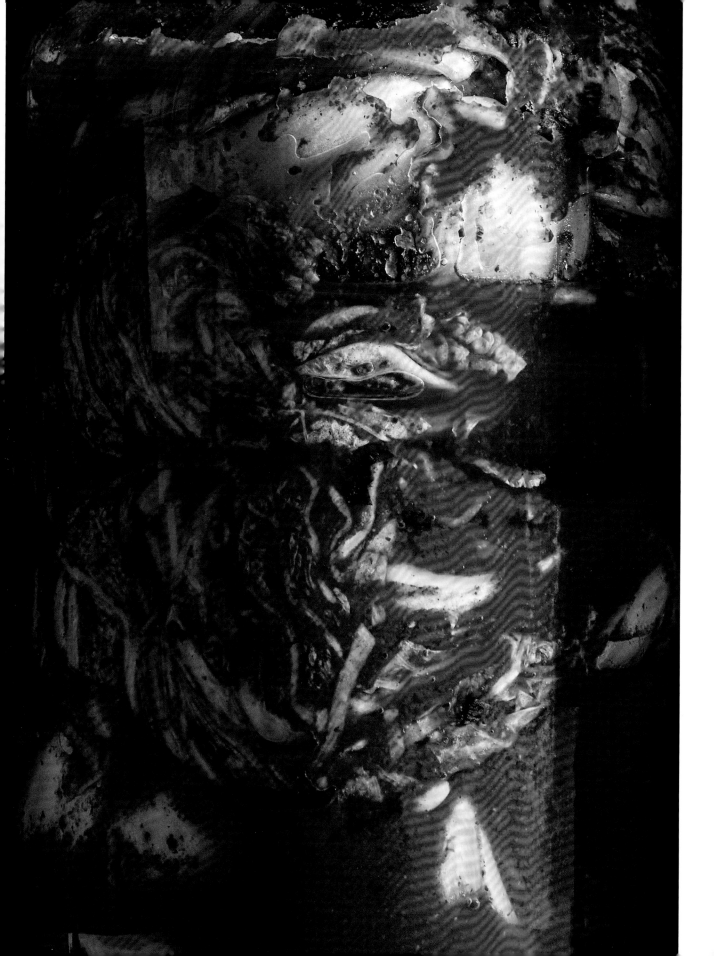

Jean's Perfect Jar of Kimchi

I would argue that this is the most important recipe in the book. Again, there are other kimchis beyond this spicy napa cabbage variety, but if you're to make just one recipe within these pages, I would start with this one. Set aside about four hours for the project, most of which is inactive time, and it'll take a couple weeks for the kimchi to ferment, too. There's a lot of waiting. But if you make this kimchi now, you'll be able to cook a thousand other things with it later, like kimchi jjigae (page 98), the homiest of Korean stews, and kimchi fried rice (page 136), the pinnacle of Korean comfort food. Consider this recipe the key that unlocks all the other levels of Korean home cooking (or at least the ones in this book).

Jean worked especially hard to get this recipe to fit a one-gallon jar *exactly* with her tong baechu kimchi, or whole napa cabbage kimchi (where the leaves are kept together by the core, rather than chopped up into pieces first; in my opinion, this results in a much better-tasting ferment). She did this mostly out of obsessiveness, but also because: Is there anything more satisfying than a recipe that makes one perfect jar of a really good thing?

There were some weeks when she was testing this recipe once a day. That's five pounds of kimchi, *every* single day. My breath smelled like garlic for months (it was wonderful). She'd tweak things here and there, take ingredients out, add them back in. Ultimately, some hard decisions were made. Ordinarily, for instance, you would cook up a mixture of water and glutinous rice flour to make a slurry, which adds bulk to the kimchi sauce and allows you to cover all the cabbage leaves evenly. At one point she was using a grated potato in place of the glutinous rice flour, which actually worked really well and tasted great. But everything changed when she developed a version without any starches at all, just to see what would happen. Not only did skipping the slurry make the recipe significantly easier; it made the kimchi taste better and more concentrated in flavor, as well.

It was fun watching Jean perfect her own signature kimchi, a recipe she can now call The One. Not least because a Korean mother's kimchi is her bread and butter, her secret sauce. In it lies all of her powers, decades of experience and Korean mom secrets. There's a saying in Korean culture that if your kimchi is good, then all your cooking is good. It's what makes your kimchi jjigae and kimchi fried rice taste the way they do.

Jean made her best jar of kimchi yet on March 5, 2021. There was a Post-it note on it. It's the kimchi you see in a lot of the photos throughout this book. We used it because it was the brightest, reddest, and most flavorful one. The resulting recipe—which is printed right here—is in many ways an extension of my mother, a family heirloom she's choosing to pass down to us. So please take care of it, use it wisely, and share it with the people you love most. And call your mom.

1 cup kosher salt

2 medium heads napa cabbage (about 2 pounds each), any dirty outer leaves removed, quartered lengthwise (see Korean Mom Tip, page 70)

FOR THE PERFECT SAUCE

½ medium yellow onion, peeled

½ medium red apple, peeled

½ medium Korean pear (aka Asian pear), peeled

10 large garlic cloves, peeled

1-inch piece fresh ginger, peeled

¾ cup gochugaru

½ cup fish sauce

½ cup saeujeot (salted fermented shrimp; see page 25)

3 tablespoons maesil cheong (green plum syrup; see page 22)

1 pound Korean radish, peeled and cut into matchsticks

5 large scallions, cut into ½-inch pieces

MAKES 1 GALLON (SEE NOTE, PAGE 70)

1. Fill a large, wide tub with 6 cups cold tap water. Add the salt and stir to dissolve. Add the cabbage quarters to the water, making sure the inner leaves are all soaked by spreading them open slightly. Let the cabbage sit in the water cut-side up until wilted and seasoned throughout, about 3 hours, flipping once halfway through. The bowl will fill with more water as the salt draws liquid out of the cabbages.

2. Meanwhile, make the perfect sauce: In a food processor, combine the onion, apple, Korean pear, garlic, and ginger and process until smooth. Transfer to a large bowl—like, the largest you've got—and add the gochugaru, fish sauce, salted fermented shrimp, plum syrup, radish, and scallions. Stir to combine.

3. Drain and rinse the salted cabbage quarters in the sink, running them under the cold tap and squeezing them of their excess liquid. Place one cabbage quarter in the large bowl with the sauce and smear it all over the cabbage and in between all the leaves. When it's fully slathered inside and out, gather its wide leafy ends together and lay them over its root end, like you're swaddling a baby, essentially folding the whole thing in half. Place that gorgeous new kimchi baby into a 1-gallon jar. Repeat with the rest of the cabbage quarters, snugly placing one finished and swaddled bundle after another into the jar. You should be able to fill the entire jar with this amount of kimchi. Top the jar with any remaining kimchi sauce and loosely close with a lid.

4. You can start eating this kimchi as soon as you make it, though it won't gain its characteristic sourness until you let it sit. To do so: Store it at room temperature until it begins to ferment and sour, 2 to 3 days depending on the season and temperature of your kitchen. Refrigerate it after that for 2 to 3 weeks until fermented and up to 6 to 8 months.

RECIPE CONTINUES

Korean Mom Tip

When quartering napa cabbages, there's a way to make your leaves look natural and ruffled (versus straight and narrow from a sharp knife cut). Jean suggests carving a 2-inch-deep cross into the root end of the cabbage to start it off and then, from there, spreading the rest of the head apart with your hands so the leaves can separate organically like *assassassa*—

"Like WHAT?" I asked, as she showed me the motion.

"*Assassassassassa*," she repeated. (This is the sound that cabbage leaves make when they're being torn into quarters, apparently.)

It's 7 in the morning and we're both cackling at the kitchen table with our coffees. I love how onomatopoeic the Korean language is. There's a word for every sound.

Note To house your kimchi while it ferments, the best option is a one-gallon glass jar with a loose-fitting plastic lid. You can find this online and at any Asian grocery store. A stainless-steel jar with a metal lid comes in close second. The one thing you should *not* use is a mason jar with an airtight lid. When it comes to kimchi, the air needs somewhere to escape—to "fart," as I like to say.

In fact, whatever jar you're using, you'll want to check on your kimchi in its early stages, every 2 to 3 days, by opening the lid and taking a sterile utensil to press down on the top of the kimchi to release some gas. This isn't entirely necessary, but it's a useful way to get to know the fermentation process and how things work in your kitchen. It's also added insurance. Your jar *could* explode (though that's never happened in my lifetime, nor in my mother's, so I don't know why it keeps happening to people).

Variation: Baek Kimchi with Beet

This hot-pink dream of a kimchi tastes incredibly refreshing and looks so beautiful, like a Vermeer painting. My mother thought it up one morning while juicing a beet.

To make it, follow the recipe for Jean's Perfect Jar of Kimchi (page 68), with these changes: Nix the gochugaru in the sauce and replace with 2 Asian probiotic yogurt drinks (such as Maeil Biofeel or Yakult) and ½ large beet (about 6 ounces), peeled and cut into very thin matchsticks. Watch with glee as the kimchi turns pinker and pinker the longer it ferments.

RECIPE CONTINUES

Variation: Bitter (in a Good Way) Green Cabbage Kimchi

I love the pleasurable bitterness of green cabbage in kimchi form. It's like baechu kimchi's long-lost cousin from the wrong side of the tracks. (But we have to admit that "wrong" sometimes tastes right, right?) Maybe it's the edginess, or the risk: Bitter used to signify to our bodies that something was dangerous to eat, but slowly, we've evolved to understand "the world's most dangerous flavor," as the chef and cookbook author Jennifer McLagan called it, as something that could actually be very good for us.

Physiology aside, this is how my mother and many people in her generation made kimchi when they first arrived in America. It's only recently that non-Asian grocery stores started carrying the more traditional napa cabbage. Before, it was something you could only get if you were really looking for it (and we're always really looking for napa cabbage). Fast-forward to thirty years later: Now I'm a green cabbage fiend, and Jean is also a born-again fan of this variation. Because the texture and flavor of green cabbage is so different from napa cabbage, we enjoy eating this one like a crunchy salad, which means you don't necessarily have to wait for it to ferment.

To make it, follow the recipe for Jean's Perfect Jar of Kimchi (page 68) with these changes: Swap out the napa cabbage for 2 heads green cabbage (about 4 pounds), quartered lengthwise. To the sauce, add 1 Asian probiotic yogurt drink (such as Maeil Biofeel or Yakult).

Seolleongtang-Restaurant Radish Kimchi page 74

Seolleongtang-Restaurant Radish Kimchi

Some of my favorite Korean dishes are the ones named after what you're meant to eat them with. It's like they were born to be together, and in the best of circumstances, are better in summation than solo.

Case in point: this spicy, crunchy radish kimchi, which has an effervescent gochugaru sauce that happens to taste especially good with a bowl of seolleongtang (page 117). Certain restaurants, like Gammeeok in New York City, specialize in the ox-bone soup, often selling just that alongside the radish kimchi. The kimchi, which is slightly sweet and super fermented, often comes in black earthenware crocks set on the tables, and is the absolute best counter to the mild, milky bone broth. Sometimes the radish is cut up already, but I love when they're still in huge rectangular slabs to be snipped into smaller pieces with scissors right at the table. As you eat this kimchi with the soup, sometimes dunking it into the bowl, your broth will turn redder and redder, the comingled flavors crescendoing with each cumulative bite.

There's one key ingredient in seolleongtang kimchi: a little probiotic yogurt drink (the red foil-capped kind sprinkled throughout Jenny Han's teen series, *To All the Boys I've Loved Before*). It's a long-known Korean restaurant trick that Jean has started incorporating into some of her own kimchis to help jump-start the fermentation process by introducing good bacteria and to add a little sweetness. You could use this same sauce to make kimchi with smaller radish cubes (called kkakdugi) or even those gorgeous ponytail radishes known as chonggak (pictured on page 75). When it comes to radish kimchi, there's truly no limit.

3 pounds Korean radish, cut into roughly 3 × 2 × 1-inch chunks

2 tablespoons sugar

2 tablespoons kosher salt

½ Korean pear (aka Asian pear), peeled

1 small yellow onion, peeled

6 large garlic cloves, peeled

1-inch piece fresh ginger, peeled

½ cup gochugaru

¼ cup fish sauce

¼ cup saeujeot (salted fermented shrimp; see page 25)

2 tablespoons maesil cheong (green plum syrup; see page 22)

2 Asian probiotic yogurt drinks, such as Maeil Biofeel or Yakult (see Note)

MAKES 1 QUART

1. Place the radish chunks in a colander in the sink, add the sugar and salt, and toss. Set aside to drain until they become slightly pliable, about 2 hours.

2. Meanwhile, in a food processor, blend the pear, onion, garlic, ginger, gochugaru, fish sauce, salted fermented shrimp, plum syrup, and yogurt drinks. Transfer to a large bowl. Add the salted, drained radishes and toss with the sauce. Taste for seasoning, adding more shrimp for saltiness and plum syrup for sweetness as desired.

3. Transfer the radish kimchi and any accumulated juices to a quart-sized glass jar or stainless steel container with a loose-fitting lid. Airtight mason jars aren't great for this because they can explode (see Note, page 70). You can start eating this kimchi as soon as you make it, though it won't gain its characteristic sourness until you let it sit. To do so: Store it at room temperature until it begins to ferment and sour, 2 to 3 days depending on the season and temperature of your kitchen. Refrigerate it after that for 2 to 3 weeks until fermented and up to 6 to 8 months.

Note Do not use regular yogurt for this; the flavor and texture would be way off. The light sweetness of Asian probiotic yogurt drinks is perfect for kimchi, where you want balance in flavor and the added benefit of lactic bacteria, which brands like Maeil Biofeel and Yakult bring.

Naengmyeon Kimchi

There are certain dishes you grow up with but still have yet to grow into. For me, that's naengmyeon, the chewy cold noodle dish (usually buckwheat) from North Korea. The kimchi garnish often served *with* naengmyeon, on the other hand, is a dreamy wonder to me: thinly sliced ribbons of Korean radish, pickled in a sharp, fruity dressing. Some would argue that the addition of vinegar makes this less of a kimchi (a salted, fermented thing) and more of a muchim (a salad-like thing dressed with your hands). All I know is that Jean calls it naengmyeon kimchi, so I call it naengmyeon kimchi. The vinegar is important here because it lends naengmyeon kimchi's characteristic acidity, which is meant to complement the chilled noodles.

My mother keeps a small jar of this pungent, vinegary radish kimchi in the fridge so that come lunchtime, all she has to do is boil the noodles. I've noticed recently that my parents eat naengmyeon for both lunch and dinner almost as often as they eat kimchi jjigae with rice. It's a main weeknight affair in the Kim household, and we have the kimchi to match. I'll still pass on the noodles nine out of ten times, but I love the brightness of this kimchi and often eat it as a banchan with other dishes.

2 pounds Korean radish, thinly sliced into 3 × 1-inch rectangles

1 tablespoon plus 2 teaspoons kosher salt

4 large garlic cloves, finely grated

½ large red apple, peeled and finely grated

2 tablespoons distilled white vinegar

2 tablespoons maesil cheong (green plum syrup; see page 22)

2 tablespoons gochugaru

1 Asian probiotic yogurt drink, such as Maeil Biofeel or Yakult

MAKES 1 QUART

1. Place the sliced radish in a colander set over a large bowl and toss with 1 tablespoon of the salt. Let it sit about 30 minutes to drain.

2. Meanwhile, in a medium bowl, stir together the garlic, apple, vinegar, plum syrup, gochugaru, and yogurt drink.

3. Gently squeeze the drained radish to release any extra liquid, discard the liquid, and add the radish to the sauce. Toss the radish until evenly coated and transfer to a 1-quart glass jar or other container.

4. You can eat this kimchi right away or store it in the refrigerator for up to 3 months. It'll ferment slowly and gain flavor as it ages. Serve with naengmyeon (see Note) or, if you're like me, with everything other than naengmyeon.

Note Though you could make your own broth from scratch for naengmyeon, my parents buy the fresh noodles at Korean supermarkets like H Mart, where they usually come packaged with the soup in little baggies that you just have to tear open and pour into a bowl. Garnish with a hard-boiled egg and cucumber if you're feeling up to it.

Perilla Kimchi

Jean keeps a lush, potted perilla plant on her deck. It grows like wildfire in the summer and has the loveliest, most fragrant leaves, which are featured heavily in Korean cooking. A member of the mint family, perilla lends a crisp, vegetal taste to brothy dishes (like the Maeuntang on page 169 and the Pork Spare Rib Soup on page 114) and to rice dishes, too (like the Summer Albap on page 148 and the Spam and Perilla Kimbap on page 138). One of our favorite ways to eat it is raw in a ssam, or wrap, for grilled meats. The plant can be expensive to buy, so most people start it from the seed. Jean's plant is *huge* now. Walk by it and you'll smell its herbaceous perfume, a scent so strong that it's said to ward off deer and other hungry pests. Once it catches on, perilla grows plentifully, and much like other bumper crops, gardeners take joy in sharing its bounty. My mom's plant isn't at that level yet, but it is a dream of hers to have a garden filled with perilla—enough for her to make perilla kimchi *and* enough to share the leaves far and wide with neighbors and friends.

When Jean showed me how to make this kimchi, I couldn't believe how simple and freeform it was. "Oh, that's it?" Of course, that's not *it*. There's a lot to a really great perilla kimchi, including the sauce and the careful layering of the leaves. Growing up, Jean's mother wouldn't make perilla kimchi like this because she was too busy working. Though this version is easy, it does require a little patience: You mix up the sauce and then have to spread it on each perilla leaf, layering the leaves as if you're making a mille-feuille. It's not especially hard, it just takes a commitment to repetitive action. Luckily, this kind of mindless monotony can be comforting. One shortcut is to layer the sauce every three leaves so that you can get through the pile faster. I actually like this method better anyway because the thin, diaphanous leaves end up tasting less salty. The point of perilla kimchi is that no matter how you make it, it will be very flavorful, and very seasoned. Which is why you would never just eat this on its own; it's meant to be banchan, countered by something soft and bland like rice. As Jean told me once, while taking a container of perilla kimchi out of her kimchi fridge to feed me: "You need to be someone who loves rice in order to enjoy this banchan."

RECIPE CONTINUES

3 ounces fresh perilla leaves
(about 2 bundles)

2 tablespoons soy sauce

1½ tablespoons fish sauce

1 tablespoon gochugaru

1 tablespoon maesil cheong
(green plum syrup; see
page 22)

1½ teaspoons sugar

2 large garlic cloves, thinly sliced

2 large scallions, minced

2 teaspoons sesame seeds

MAKES ABOUT 3 CUPS

1. Rinse the perilla leaves in a tub of water in the sink, making sure each leaf has been properly rinsed. Dry the perilla very well, either in a salad spinner or in a colander.

2. In a small bowl, mix together the soy sauce, fish sauce, gochugaru, plum syrup, sugar, garlic, scallions, and sesame seeds. This seasoning paste should be fairly thick but spreadable.

3. Take 3 perilla leaves, stack them, and use a spoon to spread a thin layer of the seasoning paste on top. It will sort of feel like you're painting a large surface with a tiny amount of paint, which is fine; you can

be pretty lazy about it. Just make sure you spread it thinly, as using too much will make it too salty. Repeat this for all of the leaves, continually layering one 3-layer batch on top of the next like a perilla trifle, lasagna, or baklava: 3 perilla leaves, thin layer of seasoning paste, 3 perilla leaves, thin layer of seasoning paste, etc.

4. Pack the stack into a shallow 3-cup container with an airtight lid. Leave it out at room temperature for 1 day to ferment and sour slightly, and then pop it in the fridge for up to 2 months. To eat, grab one leaf at a time, separating it from the stack, and lay the leaf flat over whatever you're eating, be it a bowl of rice, noodles, whatever.

Oi Sobagi

This recipe was especially difficult to pry out of the Tiger's mouth, not least because these gorgeous stuffed cucumbers require some knifework. Words like julienned, chopped, and finely grated mean something to me, as do timing cues to know when something is done. But as is her way, Jean kept using Korean onomatopoeias to describe her process.

In case you were wondering what the recipe looked like before I translated it, you will need to cut your scallions *song-song-song-song* (that's the sound of the knife chopping them). Then, you have to blanch the cucumbers in salt water until they become *kkodeul-kkodeul*, the sound of their rubbery, pliable skins (this pliability is necessary so you can open them up to fill them with the garlic chives, scallions, and carrots).

As if that weren't enough, my mother and I have very different conceptions of time, even. When I asked her how long to blanch the cucumbers, she just said, very quickly, "*1-2-3-4-5*."

"That's not real time," I said. "This is real time: 1 Mississippi, 2 Mississippi, 3 Mississippi . . . That long?"

No, like this: "*1-2-3-4-5!*"

"Mom, that's not real time . . ."

"Well, that's *my* time."

RECIPE CONTINUES

½ cup kosher salt

2½ pounds Korean or English hothouse cucumbers

3 ounces garlic chives (see Note), chopped into ½-inch pieces

2 large scallions, halved lengthwise, then cut crosswise into ½-inch lengths

½ carrot, coarsely shredded

3 large garlic cloves, finely grated

2 tablespoons gochugaru

3 tablespoons saeujeot (salted fermented shrimp; see page 25)

1 tablespoon fish sauce

2 tablespoons maesil cheong (green plum syrup; see page 22)

½ tablespoon sugar

SERVES 4 TO 6

1. In a large pot, bring 6 cups water to a boil and stir in the salt to dissolve. Blanch the cucumbers in this salted hot water one at a time until they turn bright green, anywhere from 3 to 10 seconds each (English hothouse cucumbers may need the longer time). Transfer to a cutting board and let cool completely.

2. Cut the cooled, blanched cucumbers into 3-inch lengths, then score one cut side of each length with a crisscross pattern about two-thirds of the way down into each cucumber piece (leaving 1 inch at the bottom untouched to keep them together).

3. In a small bowl, stir together the garlic chives, scallions, carrot, garlic, gochugaru, salted fermented shrimp, fish sauce, plum syrup, and sugar and carefully stuff this mixture into the scored cucumbers, using your fingers to push it down. Squeeze the stuffed cucumbers once with your hands before laying them on their sides in a large airtight container.

4. You can eat these fresh like little bundles of salad or let them ferment at room temperature for 1 day, then store them in the refrigerator to eat within the week.

Note Garlic chives have a pungent, grassy flavor (and yes, taste like garlic). They're very particular to this recipe and to Jean, not least because she grows them in her garden. You can get them at any Korean or Asian grocery store, but if you can't find them, milder chives would work in a pinch.

Spam, Kimchi, and Cabbage Stir-Fry

My mom used to make a version of this when I was younger. I've since added crunchy green cabbage for bulk, but also for flavor. I love the way it almost becomes kimchi-like by osmosis, just by existing within the same pan as the kimchi (which of course is also made from cabbage). It's sort of similar to what happens when you add porcini mushrooms to regular button mushrooms; the former lends its muskiness to the latter, spreading the love and making the overall dish taste even more balanced. The Spam is salty, so the cabbage really helps with that. Also, cabbage just rules and we should all eat more of it.

1 tablespoon toasted sesame oil

6 ounces Spam (½ can), cut into ¼-inch-thick 1-inch squares

1 cup roughly chopped store-bought or homemade kimchi (page 68)

½ small head green cabbage (about 12 ounces), cored and cut into 2-inch pieces

½ large red onion, thickly sliced

2 teaspoons gochugaru

2 teaspoons soy sauce

½ teaspoon sugar

Cooked white rice (page 128), for serving

SERVES 2

1. Heat a large skillet over medium-high heat and add the sesame oil and Spam. Cook, stirring occasionally, until slightly crispy at the edges, 2 to 3 minutes.

2. Add the kimchi and stir-fry until fragrant and starting to caramelize at the edges, another 2 to 3 minutes. Add the cabbage and onion and cook, stirring occasionally, until they're both less raw but remain crunchy, about 5 minutes.

3. Add the gochugaru, soy sauce, and sugar and stir to combine. Taste for seasonings and adjust accordingly (more gochugaru if it needs more fire, more soy if it needs more salt, and more sugar if it needs more balance).

4. Serve with white rice.

Kimchi Sandwiches

My cousin Semi remembers eating kimchi sandwiches on family picnics. The funny thing is, I don't remember these at all, and neither does her mom, my Aunt Georgia. But according to Semi, Aunt Georgia always brought sandwiches made of chopped kimchi stuffed between two slices of white bread, and the kids would eat them. I loved this image so much that I tried the sandwich myself . . . and it was interesting! (Sorry, Aunt Georgia.)

The idea still intrigued me, though. One of my favorite sandwiches is bread-and-butter pickles with butter on soft, white sandwich bread. So I tried this with kimchi and butter. Though it was a *little* better, I found that the tang of mayonnaise worked best with the fermented flavors of the filling, made even more complex and delicious when balanced with sugar and a splash of sesame oil. This is a very simple sandwich—as the best ones often are.

1 cup finely chopped drained napa cabbage kimchi, store-bought or homemade (page 68)

½ teaspoon sugar

2 teaspoons toasted sesame oil

2 tablespoons mayonnaise

4 slices soft white sandwich bread (Milk Bread with Maple Syrup, page 251, is especially good)

MAKES 2 SANDWICHES

In a small bowl, stir together the kimchi, sugar, and sesame oil. Spread the mayonnaise on two slices of bread. Divide the kimchi mixture between the two slices and top with the remaining bread slices. Cut off the crusts (optional) and slice the sandwiches in half before packing for lunch or eating.

KOREAN AMERICAN

Kimchi Bibimguksu
with Grape Tomatoes

Another favorite (and regular) raw kimchi preparation in my family is this bibimguksu, which just means "mixed noodles." For a cold noodle dish, this one is surprisingly comforting. I was testing it in the summer when Jean's garden tomatoes were at their peak, so I added them and loved the fresh pops of umami they lent. Thick-skinned grape tomatoes are best here for their snap, but you can use whatever you like. My dad loves this.

6 ounces somyeon or other thin wheat noodles

2 large eggs

1 tablespoon gochugaru

1 tablespoon sugar

1 tablespoon toasted sesame oil

1 tablespoon toasted sesame seeds

½ cup finely chopped drained napa cabbage kimchi, store-bought or homemade (page 68)

1 pint grape tomatoes, halved

1 small cucumber (doesn't matter what kind), julienned, for serving

SERVES 2

1. Bring a medium pot of water to a boil and cook the somyeon according to package directions (usually about 4 minutes). Drain the noodles and rinse under cold water. Set aside.

2. Fill the same pot with water and bring it to a boil over high heat. Add the eggs carefully and reduce the heat to medium-low to gently simmer for 6 to 7 minutes (this yields a soft-boiled egg). Using a slotted spoon, bring the eggs over to the sink and run them under cold water so you can grab them with your hands and tap the bottoms against the counter or other hard surface to crack the shell. Quickly run this under cold water again (the temperature shock will cause the egg white to contract slightly away from its shell, making it easier to peel). Peel the eggs and set aside.

3. In a large bowl, whisk together the gochugaru, sugar, sesame oil, and sesame seeds. Toss the kimchi in this mixture and add the noodles and tomatoes. Use your hands to mix everything together so the noodles are evenly coated in the kimchi dressing.

4. To serve, divide the noodles and tomatoes between two bowls. Slice each egg in half and top the noodles with the eggs and julienned cucumber.

Bacon-Fat Kimchi Jeon
with Herbs

As long as you have kimchi in the house, a meal can be made. Case in point: kimchi jeon, pancakes made primarily from chopped kimchi, kimchi juice, and a little flour. While jeon is often considered a party food, kimchi jeon has always been an everyday staple in our family. These versions seem fancy with the pressed-in parsley and bacon fat, but they're actually pretty quick to throw together and taste wonderful with white rice. You could dip these in soy sauce and rice vinegar; that's what we normally would do. But I've come to appreciate with equal fervor a midnight snack of cold kimchi jeon slathered with sour cream and dill.

FOR THE DIPPING SAUCE

1 tablespoon soy sauce

1 tablespoon rice vinegar

Pinch of sesame seeds

Pinch of gochugaru

1 large scallion, thinly sliced on the diagonal

FOR THE JEON

4 slices thick-cut bacon, finely chopped

2 tablespoons olive oil

1 cup finely chopped drained napa cabbage kimchi, store-bought or homemade (page 68)

¼ cup kimchi juice

1 large egg

1 tablespoon gochugaru

1 cup all-purpose flour

1 tablespoon sugar

Pinch of kosher salt

2 large scallions, thinly sliced on the diagonal

Fresh flat-leaf parsley, dill, or mint

MAKES 6 TO 8 JEON

1. Make the dipping sauce: In a small dish, stir together the soy sauce, vinegar, sesame seeds, gochugaru, and scallion. Set aside.

2. Make the jeon: Add the bacon and olive oil to a cold large nonstick skillet. Set the pan over medium-high heat and fry the bacon, stirring occasionally, until crispy on all sides, 3 to 4 minutes. Remove the bacon with a slotted spoon to a plate lined with paper towels. Transfer the bacon fat to a small dish, leaving 1 tablespoon in the pan to fry the first batch of jeon.

3. Meanwhile, in a medium bowl, stir together the kimchi, kimchi juice, ½ cup water, the egg, gochugaru, flour, sugar, salt, and scallions.

4. Heat the pan with the bacon fat over high heat. Ladle about ¼ cup of the batter into the hot fat. You should be able to fit 2 to 3 jeon in the pan at a time. As they fry on the first side, neatly lay the parsley on top and press down slightly so the leaves stick. Sprinkle some of the reserved cooked bacon on top. Fry until lightly browned and crispy, about 2 minutes per side, then transfer the jeon to a large platter while you cook the rest of the batter, adding more bacon fat to the pan between batches.

5. These are best eaten as soon as they come off the heat. Serve with the dipping sauce.

Caramelized-Kimchi Baked Potatoes

If sugar on baked potatoes sounds weird to you, then maybe you haven't tried it. It's something Jean always did at buffets. She'd load her baked potato up with the usual: a little sour cream, some cheese, and chives (or whatever was available at the buffet), and then, her pièce de résistance, sugar from one of those packets sitting on the table meant for coffee. Because of her, my brother and I always sugar our baked potatoes slightly; it adds balance, especially here with caramelized kimchi and nutty sesame oil. My mother loves this baked potato and so do I, not least because it feels like a full meal. You could serve it alongside a side salad or eat it as is. If you want to make a large party platter of baked-stuffed potatoes (à la the *New York Times* reporter Priya Krishna and her mother, Ritu), then use smaller spuds.

4 large Korean yellow or Yukon Gold potatoes (about 2 pounds)

4 slices thick-cut bacon (about 4 ounces), chopped

1 tablespoon toasted sesame oil

1 cup finely chopped napa cabbage kimchi, store-bought or homemade (page 68)

Sugar

1 cup shredded mozzarella cheese, for serving

Sour cream, for serving

Chopped chives, for serving

MAKES 4 POTATOES

1. Preheat the oven to 400°F.

2. Arrange the potatoes on a sheet pan and bake until fluffy and tender on the inside (when checked with a paring knife) and crispy on the outside, about 1 hour.

3. In a medium skillet, fry the bacon over medium-high heat until crispy, about 4 minutes. Use a slotted spoon to transfer to a plate lined with paper towels to drain. Set aside.

4. At this point you can drain some of the bacon fat if there's a lot more than 1 tablespoon (but usually I just leave it). With the pan still over medium-high heat, add the sesame oil and carefully nestle in the kimchi (it may splatter). Season with a pinch of sugar. Stirring occasionally, cook until the kimchi is caramelized and fragrant, 2 to 3 minutes. Set aside to cool slightly.

5. When the potatoes are done, let them cool slightly before handling (or not, if you're like Jean and somehow have heatproof hands). Cut a lengthwise slit down the center of each potato and gently press the two ends together with your fingers to widen the slit. Use a fork to fluff up the inside of each potato.

6. Now, load them up: First sprinkle some more sugar into each potato (just trust me!). Then top with the mozzarella (it should melt slightly from the heat of the potato), caramelized kimchi, sour cream, cooked bacon pieces, and chives.

Kimchi-Braised Short Ribs
with Pasta

Kimchi jjim is one of the best dishes in Jean's culinary canon, if you ask me. I've taken her base method for braised kimchi and added short ribs to it, though you could replace the beef with a gorgeous pork shoulder. This is a great example of kimchi in its last state: cooked down and absolutely melting. You can eat the kimchi in this dish with a spoon, though you might not even find it after the meat has been shredded and threaded around long, luscious pappardelle noodles and showered with cheese. Serve with a side salad if you wish, or nothing.

1½ pounds English-cut, bone-in beef short ribs

Kosher salt and freshly ground black pepper

Olive oil

2 cups roughly chopped napa cabbage kimchi, store-bought or homemade (page 68)

½ large yellow onion, thinly sliced

4 large garlic cloves, peeled

3 tablespoons gochugaru

2 tablespoons soy sauce

1 tablespoon sugar

1 tablespoon toasted sesame oil

1 pound pappardelle or other wide pasta noodles

Finely chopped fresh parsley

Wedge of Parmesan cheese, for serving

SERVES 4 TO 6

1. Preheat the oven to 325°F.

2. Season the short ribs generously with salt and pepper. Heat a large Dutch oven over medium-high heat. Add enough olive oil to coat the bottom of the pot and then add the short ribs, searing until browned on both sides, about 8 minutes total. Use tongs to transfer the short ribs to a plate.

3. To the pot, add the kimchi, onion, garlic, gochugaru, soy sauce, sugar, sesame oil, and 2 cups water. Stir together, bring to a simmer, and nestle the ribs back in, bone-side up, making sure they're mostly covered if not completely covered by the liquid.

4. Cover the pot, transfer to the oven, and bake until the short ribs are meltingly tender (the meat should fall off the bone when poked with a fork or spoon), the liquid has reduced by about half, and the kimchi and onions have melted into jammy submission, 2½ to 3 hours.

5. Remove the pot from the oven and use a spoon or ladle to skim the fat from the surface. Carefully remove the short ribs and any bones that may have slipped out. Discard the bones and shred the meat with two forks. Return the meat to the pot.

6. Meanwhile, bring a large pot of generously salted water to a boil. Add the pappardelle and cook until nearly al dente according to the package directions, chopping off a couple minutes so you can finish cooking the pasta in the sauce. Using tongs, transfer the pasta from the pasta cooking pot directly to the Dutch oven with the sauce and meat and set over medium heat. Use tongs to toss the sauce with the pasta until the sauce reduces, becomes thicker and richer, and coats the pasta thinly, about 5 minutes. Taste for seasoning, adding more salt and pepper as needed.

7. To serve, add as much parsley to the pasta as you'd like (I like a lot) and toss.

8. Plate the pasta, making sure each plate gets short-rib meat. Finely grate some Parmesan over each plate, leaving the block of cheese on the table with the grater so guests can help themselves to more.

S Is for Stew

The Korean art of gentle boiling

My cousin Semi used to be a line cook at a restaurant in Nashville. One day, in between shifts, the executive chef called upon the entire staff to develop their own original braised dishes to cook in an *Iron Chef*–style competition. The winning braise would be added to the menu. Semi made her take on kalbijjim, thick English-cut short ribs braised in a salty-sweet soy sauce and studded with comforting root vegetables. First, she boiled the ribs to remove the fat and scum from the meat (because that's how her mother, my aunt Georgia, does it), then continued to boil them for an hour or two more until they were meltingly soft. If you've ever tasted kalbijjim—or had Semi's cooking—then you won't be surprised that she won the competition and her dish was added to the menu.

But her colleagues put up a fit: "We thought this was a braising competition," they said. "Semi *boiled* her meat." Semi didn't think anything of it. Boiling is what she was taught. "It's a different method," she told me. "The people who complained about my win went to culinary school and learned French techniques. But all the sous-chefs and even the executive chef picked my stew." Beyond that, the chef also listened when Semi explained exactly how she made the beef so tender and the sauce so balanced. Asking no further questions, the chef said, "Cool. We're doing it like that."

The definition of *braise* is "to cook slowly in fat and a small amount of liquid in a closed pot"—the liquid and the closed pot being key here. It's a common misconception that braising necessarily means low heat, which is why this chapter will include high-heat recipes that use what I believe to be a very beautiful, quintessentially Korean technique: gentle boiling. In cooking, if there's a rapid simmer and a rolling boil, then I'd place the gentle boil in between those. In a gentle boil, the bubbles are brisk and vociferous, but controlled and even—there should be no chance of bubbling over. Look for something between small bubbles and big bubbles that are quick to pop. An added reminder that boiling, i.e., 212°F, is a notch above simmering. And while simmering is still useful for long, drawn-out soups (like the Sunday-Night Chicken Sujebi on page 110 or the Cornish Game Hen Soup on page 106), for quick weeknight stews like A Very Good Kimchi Jjigae (page 98) and the canned meat–bejeweled Budae Jjigae (page 101), gentle boiling can be *the* secret to unlocking the best in a pot of braised food.

The other secret to Korean braises is how you layer in flavor. While developing these recipes, my mother wouldn't stop talking about how a pinch of Dasida (a Korean brand of MSG-rich soup base powder) would "bring all the flavors together." But she restrained herself because experienced cooks like her know how to reproduce those umami qualities with natural ingredients and particular steps. Scallions, for instance, are more than just garnish here; they're essential flavoring (see page 103). And gentle boiling ensures that you're extracting marrow from bones (like in the Seolleongtang Noodles with Scallion Gremolata on page 117 or the Pork Spare Rib Soup in the Style of Gamjatang on page 114) and that you're *just* blanching fresh, crunchy vegetables (like in the Doenjang Jjigae with Silken Tofu and Raw Zucchini on page 104).

A final idiosyncratic note to mention is that Koreans rarely sear their meat before a braise, not least because there are so many other avenues toward flavor. For Semi, the point of searing is to achieve that hard crust. But when you're boiling a tough cut of meat over a long period of time, you just won't benefit from that seared section of protein (and frankly won't taste the difference with all the other bold pantry ingredients often found in Korean braises). Especially in the case of the Kalbijjim with Root Vegetables and Beef-Fat Croutons (page 122), the braised short rib meat is velvety and absolutely falls apart, like an oversized flannel draping an armchair, which is precisely why you don't actually want that hard crust. I've always felt that it can often feel like an unnecessary step that many American home cooks do without thinking because someone once told them they had to do it. But there are so many ways to cook good food. Why restrict ourselves to just one way?

A Very Good Kimchi Jjigae

According to Jean, a good kimchi jjigae, or kimchi stew, starts with good kimchi. Sounds obvious enough. The idea is that if you have a ripe, well-fermented batch of kimchi to start with, then you don't need much else to flavor the body of this very basic stew—arguably the most popular of Korean jjigaes. When my mother cooks this, she relies on the natural kimchi juice of her mukeunji, a very old, very ripe kimchi, to season the entire dish (no added salt or seasonings). But even I don't always have a great, homemade kimchi on hand like that, which is why this recipe accounts for any lack of ambrosial Korean-mom stash, fortifying the stew with gochujang and gochugaru, which add body, color, and heat; and fish sauce, which lends that quintessential lip-smacking savoriness. Stir-frying the gochugaru-dusted pork belly in a little butter first ensures that the resultant stew has a layer of glorious red-pepper oil floating atop the other bits and bobs.

6 ounces boneless, skinless pork belly, cut into 1-inch pieces

2 large garlic cloves, finely grated

1 tablespoon gochugaru, plus more to taste

Pinch of kosher salt, plus more to taste

1 tablespoon unsalted butter

1 cup roughly chopped napa cabbage kimchi, store-bought or homemade (page 68)

½ cup kimchi juice

1 tablespoon gochujang

1 teaspoon fish sauce

½ medium yellow onion, thinly sliced

1 daepa or 2 large scallions, thinly sliced on the diagonal, for garnish

Cooked white rice (page 128), for serving

SERVES 2

1. In a small bowl, toss the pork belly with the garlic, gochugaru, and salt.

2. In a small pot, melt the butter over medium-low heat. Add the pork belly mixture and stir-fry until aromatic, just a few seconds, making sure the garlic and gochugaru don't burn. (The pork won't release much fat at this stage, so don't worry about that.)

3. Add the kimchi, kimchi juice, gochujang, fish sauce, and 1 cup water. Bring to a boil over high heat, then reduce the heat to medium-low. Cover the pot and gently boil until the kimchi has softened and the pork is cooked through, about 10 minutes.

4. Reduce the heat to low, add the onion, cover again, and simmer until the onion releases some of its natural juices, adding to the aromatic broth, about 5 minutes. Taste for seasoning, adding more salt or gochugaru as desired. Garnish with the daepa and serve with white rice.

Budae Jjigae

One way to think of budae jjigae, or "army base stew," is as an amped-up kimchi jjigae—a bubbling hodgepodge of ingredients like kimchi, Spam, hot dogs, noodles, and American cheese, a cultural by-product of leftover military rations after the Korean War. In fact, every time I make kimchi jjigae, the leftovers inevitably transmogrify into a more delicious and more complex budae jjigae over the week, as I slowly add ingredients to it, refreshing it each time with a new thinly sliced onion and a "fresh" smattering of Spam. I love the way the old Spam has soaked up all the kimchi juices (while also making the fiery broth extra flavorful with its fat and salt) and the way the new Spam breathes life into the jjigae again. For me, budae jjigae is kimchi jjigae in its ninth life.

But with its rich and complicated war history dating back to the 1950s, budae jjigae isn't celebrated by everyone. It's no wonder that some older generations of Koreans don't love this dish, whether they see it as a blot on the nation's history, a remnant of war trauma, or a recurrent reminder of hard times when food was scarce. In 1940, Bangseop Kim, my grandfather on my father's side, fled what would become North Korea for Seoul in South Korea. He lived his whole life recognizing that he had just skirted a national division that would define Korean identity forever. According to my father, Bangseop never ate canned meats like Spam, Vienna sausages, or even instant ramyun noodles—let alone the sum of these parts, budae jjigae. Maybe because it reminded him too much of a world he thought he had escaped.

Years later, my mom and dad, less directly affected by the traumata of that war, would go to college and order budae jjigae at restaurants, where it was quite expensive. Even today, they still consider it a luxury meal. Because here's the thing: Despite its thrifty countenance, to make this stew requires the purchase of a slew of the supermarket's most expensive canned meats. People don't realize that Spam can cost upwards of 4 to 5 dollars depending on where you're shopping. In America especially, Spam has a wrongfully déclassé reputation, which was difficult for me as a Korean American who grew up considering it a great comfort food, a link between two countries I straddle. For context, in Korea, people gift huge packages of Spam. But for every bad thing, there's a good thing: For my grandmother Hyunseok, who lived through the Korean War and married

RECIPE CONTINUES

early to avoid becoming a comfort woman for the Japanese Army, budae jjigae tells the story not just of hardship and pain, but of resourcefulness, as well. It tells the story of my grandmother's survival.

Ultimately, then, budae jjigae is, for my family and me, a celebration stew. It's a really delicious way to feed a large crowd in one fell swoop, with mostly pantry ingredients. All you need is the pot, a ladle, and a few bowls of white rice to soak up all the accoutrements, a landing pad for the cheese. Don't sleep on the rich soup, fortified with all of those incredible canned meats. It tastes special, and lived in. It helps that everyone I've ever served this dish to seems to love it, especially once you add the ramyun noodles.

FOR THE SAUCE

2 large garlic cloves, thinly sliced

2 tablespoons gochugaru

2 tablespoons gochujang

2 tablespoons soup soy sauce (see page 23)

1 teaspoon sugar

FOR THE STEW

4 ounces Korean radish, thinly sliced into roughly 2-inch squares

½ medium yellow onion, thinly sliced

½ can Spam (about 6 ounces), thickly sliced into roughly 2-inch squares

½ pound assorted sausages, such as sweet Italian sausages, Vienna sausages, and other hot dogs, cut into bite-size pieces

4 slices thick-cut bacon, cut into bite-size pieces

1 cup roughly chopped napa cabbage kimchi, store-bought or homemade (page 68)

1 large jalapeño, halved, seeded, and thinly sliced crosswise

2 daepa or 4 large scallions, thinly sliced on the diagonal

1 package instant ramyun noodles (see Note), seasoning packs reserved for another time

1 slice American cheese

Cooked white rice (page 128), for serving

SERVES 6 TO 8

1. Make the sauce: In a small dish, stir together the garlic, gochugaru, gochujang, soup soy sauce, and sugar.

2. Make the stew: In a large, wide pot, neatly arrange—in groups—the Korean radish, onion, Spam, sausages, bacon, kimchi, jalapeño, daepa, and the prepared sauce. Add 4 cups water, set over high heat, and bring to a boil. Reduce the heat to medium-low and gently boil until the bacon and any raw sausage is cooked through, 15 to 20 minutes.

3. Add the ramyun noodles and let cook according to package directions. Blanket the slice of cheese over the cooked noodles and serve immediately with white rice.

Note The word "ramyun" refers to Korean-style instant noodles. Where Korean ramyun is always instant, Japanese ramen can be fresh or instant. The brand here doesn't matter so much. Though Shin is arguably the most popular, I enjoy the chewiness of Samyang and Jin, but use whatever you like and whatever you have on hand.

The King of Scallions (and Other Negotiables)

Writing this cookbook with Jean was very fun—and very funny. We were constantly bickering over the smallest details. The first test for a recipe usually consisted of me standing back and watching her cook it, and my job was to translate her method into measurements and exact times, and ideally as few steps as possible. The trick was deciding which ingredients and which steps were nonnegotiable—because there *were* times when she and I differed completely in opinion about how a thing should be cooked or seared or boiled or chopped. It comes down to the main difference in our culinary training: Korean versus American.

My mom will be the first to admit, though, that she doesn't always know why she does certain things, and I'm probably an ass for pressing her on them instead of blindly following like a good son. I've made a career out of writing clear, effective recipes, a culmination of years of training in this industry—but that's no match for her decades of experience cooking Korean food. I can't tell you how many random extracts and syrups (and Korean mom tips) she has up her sleeve. Luckily, even she doesn't expect me to include many of them in these recipes, so when she's really fighting me on something, I know to concede. Also: her wrath.

One magical ingredient I *will* include—because my mom seems to rely on it heavily and claims it's the secret to the natural umami in all her dishes—is daepa, a large scallion (not a leek) that she buys in bulk, chops up, and freezes in bags to throw handfuls of into whatever she's cooking. It's the king of scallions. This shows, too, how prevalent that daepa flavor is in her food. When you make the convenience version of something, then it must be pretty regular in your cooking. And yet, even the daepa is negotiable, of course. If you don't live near an H Mart or other Asian market that sells the large scallions, then you can just substitute a couple of regular-size scallions per daepa. According to my mother, the umami flavor will be more muted, but that's life sometimes.

Another ingredient that you'll notice is prevalent in this chapter: gukganjang, or soup soy sauce. It's a by-product of making the fermented soybean paste called doenjang. As its name suggests, you add it to light-colored soups to flavor them without turning them black like regular soy would, not least because it's a little saltier so you need less of it. Comparatively speaking, soup soy sauce has more savoriness, as well. But if using regular soy sauce because that's what you have, then just reduce the amount by about half and adjust the rest of the seasonings with additional salt.

Doenjang Jjigae
with Silken Tofu and Raw Zucchini

This recipe made my mom say: *"Daebak!"* (Which means: "Exceptional!") Though doenjang jjigae—a bubbling, soupy pot of doenjang (fermented soybean paste), vegetables, meat, and tofu—is one of the most basic stews in Korean cuisine, I don't feel that I've ever made a competent one until now. Not that this version is traditional by any means. In fact, it's more akin to another dish called gang doenjang, which is a saltier, richer, thicker version of doenjang jjigae. Growing up, Jean would often turn any leftover doenjang jjigae into gang doenjang, and rather than eating it as a stew, we'd enjoy it as a salty, umami-rich condiment to be stirred into white rice. That's why my recipe doesn't call for much water, instead relying on the natural sweet juices from the vegetables to thin out the stew.

My own addition, sundubu (silken tofu), really fills the meal out and tastes so sweet and wonderful with the salty, fermented flavors. The enoki mushrooms are absurdly fun to eat, kind of like noodles, and the zucchini, which I like to salt and add raw at the very end so they maintain their crunch, are full of vegetal gumption. And in case it matters to you, this stew does happen to be vegan.

1 large zucchini, diced

Kosher salt

1 teaspoon toasted sesame oil

4 tablespoons doenjang (see page 23)

1 medium yellow onion, diced

1 daepa or 2 scallions, thinly sliced on the diagonal

5 ounces enoki mushrooms, roots trimmed and separated

11 ounces sundubu (extra-soft or silken tofu), broken up into 2 to 3 large chunks

Cooked white rice (page 128), for serving

SERVES 4

1. In a medium bowl, toss together the zucchini and ½ teaspoon salt and set aside.

2. In a small pot, combine the sesame oil and doenjang and sauté over medium-low heat, stirring often, for 1 to 2 minutes until fragrant. Add the onion, daepa, and 1½ cups water and bring to a boil over high heat, then reduce the heat to medium-low. Gently boil, stirring occasionally, until the onion is translucent, the daepa are wilted, and the liquid is nearly evaporated, about 10 minutes.

3. Reduce the heat to low and stir in the mushrooms and tofu. Season with salt, cover the pot, and simmer for another 5 minutes to soften the mushrooms and warm the tofu through. The mushrooms should have released some of their liquid by now, making the thick jjigae a little saucier, the consistency of stew, not soup—though you can add more water if needed. Taste for seasoning and adjust with salt.

4. Drain the zucchini (discarding any accumulated liquid) and stir into the stew. Serve with white rice.

Cornish Game Hen Soup
with Fried-Shallot Oil

This recipe borrows from the structure of samgyetang, a soup made from small, young chickens stuffed with rice and then boiled in a rich, fortified broth. Each person gets a whole chicken, and as you eat the refreshing soup, you scoop the rice out of its cavity with your spoon and sort of tear pieces from the bird with your hands, dunking them in a seasoned shallot oil. Ordinarily this dish would be cooked with ginseng (the *sam* in samgyetang) and jujubes (red dates). But more often than not I don't have them around, so I reach for what I do have: garlic, ginger, and onions.

The real star anyway is the Cornish game hen, which many people forget exists at the grocery store. It's also what my mother used when she immigrated to America and didn't have access to the young chickens that would otherwise be used in Korea to make samgyetang. Once stuffed with glutinous sweet rice and boiled, the already tender game hens become even plumper, and the resulting broth is especially nice because you've simmered the entire beast: skin, bones, flesh, and all. This is chicken and rice at its most comforting—and it'll knock a cold right out of you.

¾ cup glutinous rice (aka sweet rice), or any other short-grain white rice

2 Cornish game hens (1 to 1½ pounds each), any giblets removed and discarded

17 large garlic cloves, peeled (see Note)

Kosher salt and ground white pepper

4-inch piece fresh ginger, thickly sliced

½ large yellow onion, halved

2 medium shallots, thinly sliced

½ cup olive oil

Fresh cilantro leaves plus tender stems, for serving

SERVES 2

1. Place the rice in a sieve and run it under the tap for a few seconds to rinse off some of the excess starch. Transfer to a small bowl and cover with water. Let soak for 10 minutes, then drain the rice in the sieve.

2. Set the Cornish hens on a cutting board and insert 5 garlic cloves into each bird's cavity. Using a spoon, divide the rice evenly between the cavities as well. (You can tie their legs together at this point with kitchen twine, but I tend to just skip this step. I don't mind a little rice escaping their cavities and thickening the lovely broth . . .)

Note Seventeen cloves of garlic: That is not a typo, and all of that garlic is absolutely imperative. This dish is yet another reason I recommend buying one of those containers of ready-peeled garlic cloves (a real staple in our Korean American household). But should you be starting from a couple fresh heads, don't hesitate to smash the cloves with the side of your knife to more easily separate them from their skins.

3. Place the stuffed hens, breast-side up, into a medium pot or saucepan (they should fit snugly). Sprinkle with 2 teaspoons salt and 1 teaspoon white pepper. Add the remaining 7 garlic cloves, ginger, and onion around the hens and fill the pot with water so the water nearly covers the hens but not completely (it's actually best that they're not fully submerged so the white meat can slowly steam in the covered pot while the dark meat braises in the soup and gets effortlessly tender). Bring the pot to a boil over high heat. Cover, reduce the heat to low, and simmer, spooning the hot broth over the breast meat a couple times during cooking, until the chickens are cooked through and super tender, about 1 hour. You'll know it's done by jiggling one leg; the meat will be so soft that the bone may fall right out.

4. Meanwhile, in a small sauce-pan, bring the shallots and olive oil to a gentle simmer over low heat. Stir occasionally until the shallots start to brown, 20 to 30 minutes. Using a slotted spoon, remove the crispy shallots and transfer to a plate lined with paper towels to drain. Season the oil with a little salt and white pepper and set aside. This will be the dipping sauce for the chicken.

5. Season the soup with additional salt and white pepper, as needed, then use two forks to transfer each hen to its own soup bowl. Divide the broth between the bowls, top with the fried shallots and fresh cilantro, and serve with the shallot-y dipping sauce.

Dakdoritang

Chicken and potato lovers can rejoice in this comforting gochujang-slicked stew, in which bone-in chicken drumsticks and Korean yellow potatoes are deeply braised in a sweet, sticky sauce of soy sauce and gochugaru. Carrots and onions contribute to the nourishing flavors here, but nothing says dakdoritang like the sweet, pillow-like yellow potatoes. They're worth it for their texture and flavor (and can be found at any Korean grocery store). But should you not be able to source the yellow potatoes in particular, a Yukon Gold will do in a pinch.

For years, some Korean critics have felt that the *dori* in dakdoritang was borrowed from the Japanese word for "bird," campaigning instead for a more modern Korean name: dakbokkeumtang (literally "stir-fried chicken soup," which this dish is not; it's braised). But recent scholarship proves that the word *dori* actually refers to the Korean word for "in pieces" (the chicken, that is). Whatever you call it—dakdoritang or dakbokkeumtang—you'll need a bowl of fresh white rice to soak up the fire. This is very spicy.

2 pounds chicken drumsticks

⅓ cup soy sauce

¼ cup gochugaru

2 tablespoons gochujang

2 tablespoons dark brown sugar

8 large garlic cloves, finely grated

1 large yellow onion, cut into 1-inch chunks

2 large Korean yellow potatoes, peeled and cut into 1-inch chunks

1 large carrot, cut into 1-inch chunks

1 large jalapeño, halved, seeded (if you're scared of spice), and thinly sliced

1 tablespoon toasted sesame oil

2 daepa or 4 large scallions, thinly sliced on the diagonal, for garnish

Cooked white rice (page 128), for serving

SERVES 4

1. Bring a large pot of water to a boil over high heat and add the chicken drumsticks, poaching them until no longer pink, about 5 minutes. (The water may not return to a boil, which is totally fine.) Drain the water, rinse the chicken under cold tap water, and return them to the empty pot.

2. In a small bowl, stir together the soy sauce, gochugaru, gochujang, brown sugar, garlic, and 1⅓ cups water and add to the pot with the chicken. Bring to a boil over high heat. Reduce the heat to medium and cook at a gentle boil until the sauce has reduced slightly, about 10 minutes.

3. Add the onion, potatoes, carrot, and jalapeño and continue gently boiling until the chicken is tender and no longer pink on the inside and the vegetables are cooked through, 20 to 30 minutes. (Test the vegetables with a fork, which should enter and exit a potato with little resistance.) Stir in the sesame oil and garnish the pot with the daepa.

4. Serve the pot of dakdoritang in the center of the table, family-style, with a ladle and bowls of white rice.

Sunday-Night Chicken Sujebi

I've always believed that you can never have enough chicken soup recipes up your sleeve. This one is a bit of a mash-up between the stock I make after picking the meat off of a Sunday roast chicken (page 210) and sujebi, a Korean soup ordinarily made with anchovy broth and thin, chewy pieces of kneaded flour dough that gets torn into the pot by hand. Sujebi comes from the Korean words for "hand," *su*, and "fold," *jeop* (in case that clears anything up for you). All I know is that I used to help my mom shape these cute little dough flakes. I don't know if it's the ½ cup of potato starch or the kneading—or just the proportions of her sujebi dough recipe—but Jean's dumplings are the chewiest and, for me, the best.

In this interpretation of sujebi, I wanted to replace the mild anchovy broth with a more heavily seasoned, fortified chicken stock perfumed with bay leaves—like, lots of them, crushed into pieces so you get their full effect (I hate when recipes call for just one or two). No need to peel the onion and carrots, by the way; their skins will lend color and flavor, and everything gets strained out in the end anyway. As the flour pieces cook in the chicken-y liquid and become tenderly distended, floating to the top like little life rafts and thickening the already wonderful soup, I can't help but be reminded of the many plates of chicken and dumplings I ate at various Cracker Barrels on road trips through the American South.

FOR THE SOUP

1 whole chicken (4 to 5 pounds), cut into 10 serving pieces

1 large yellow onion, thickly sliced

2 large celery stalks, thickly sliced, plus leaves for garnish

1 large carrot, thickly sliced

4 dried bay leaves, crushed with your hands

7 large garlic cloves, smashed with the side of a knife

1 tablespoon black peppercorns

Kosher salt

FOR THE SUJEBI DOUGH

½ cup potato starch

1½ cups all-purpose flour

1 large egg

Pinch of kosher salt

SERVES 4 TO 6

1. Make the soup: In a large soup pot or Dutch oven, add the chicken, onion, celery, carrot, bay leaves, garlic, and peppercorns. Lightly season with salt (you can add more later), cover the chicken completely with water, and bring to a boil over high heat. Reduce the heat to low, cover, and gently simmer until the broth deepens in flavor and the chicken becomes effortlessly tender, almost falling apart, about 2 hours.

RECIPE CONTINUES

2. Meanwhile, make the sujebi dough: In a large bowl, with a fork or chopsticks, stir together ½ cup cold tap water, the potato starch, flour, egg, and salt until combined and formed into a rough dough. At this point you can switch to your hands and knead the dough directly in the bowl (or on the counter). Using the heel of your palm, push against the dough away from you and pull it back onto itself, like you're constantly folding it in half while simultaneously pressing down. (What you're doing here is creating gluten, which results in the most pleasurable chewiness.) Do this for about 5 minutes until the dough ball is smooth. Cover with plastic wrap and set aside while you finish the soup.

3. Set a colander over a large bowl and carefully strain the soup. Once the chicken cools enough to handle, pick out the chicken pieces from the colander, shred the meat into bite-size pieces, and return to the pot. Discard the spent bones, vegetables, and herbs.

4. Pour the now strained, beautiful broth you've worked so hard on (good job!) into the pot over the chicken. You should have about 10 cups. Bring the broth to a boil over high heat. Start tearing small 1-inch pieces of dough from the dough ball and, using your fingers, stretch them out until uniformly thin all over. (You should be able to hold the dough flakes up to the light and see it shine through.) As you make these little dough flakes, toss them into the boiling soup and cook the dough until they float to the top and the flour is no longer raw, 5 to 10 minutes.

5. Taste the broth for seasoning (does it need more salt or pepper?), garnish with the celery leaves, and serve immediately.

Tip When storing leftovers of this soup, be sure to separate the sujebi from its broth (use a slotted spoon to store them in another airtight container), or else the former will absolutely soak up the latter and make the elixir that you've worked so hard to create disappear.

On Soaking and Blanching Meat

As Jean and I were developing this chapter's recipes, my aim was to produce delicious, streamlined results with as few steps as possible. Her goal, on the other hand, seemed always to be: how to remove the gamey flavor from these cuts of meat. Korean cooks often soak their red meat before cooking it. And even before fully cooking it, they sometimes blanch their meat first as well, then discard the water before proceeding with the soup, stew, braise, what have you. My mother has done this her whole life—and I never believed it made much of a difference until we cooked through these recipes together and tasted everything side by side.

Mom knows best, of course, but I've arrived at a sort of middle ground (especially as someone who ordinarily tends to enjoy the natural iron-red flavor of meat): In some recipes, such as the Pork Spare Rib Soup (page 114) and the Seolleongtang Noodles (page 117), the blanching step certainly results in a cleaner-tasting broth, which is desirable in those dishes. And in the case of the soups or stews with short ribs, I found that soaking the meat beforehand really did make for a less muddied end result in terms of flavor, though the blanching step didn't seem to make much of an additional difference, not to mention you ended up losing out on some really great beef broth.

In short, in some recipes, these additional steps do make a strong impact on the final outcome of the dishes and greatly improved them, but I don't live by blanket statements, and in this case, too, I don't think you need to do each step all the time. So rest assured: If a recipe calls for soaking or blanching the meat, know that we took the extra steps very seriously and only included them where we truly felt there was a big difference in quality.

Pork Spare Rib Soup
in the Style of Gamjatang

Gamjatang is an aromatic soup traditionally made with marrow-rich pork neck bones and potatoes. *Gamja* means "potato" in Korean, but what some don't know is that it's also the name of a specific pork bone along the animal's neck. Thus, gamjatang is named after the bones, not the potatoes.

My mother is not usually one for shortcuts, and certainly not any that could dilute the end result. But in the case of this dish, which is our take on gamjatang, we decided to swap the neck bones for fleshy spare ribs—for a few reasons: First, the broth is so heavily flavored with seasonings (including all *three* mother jangs: ganjang, gochujang, and doenjang; see pages 22–23) that we felt the difference in end taste was minimal between the neck bone version and the spare rib version. Second, the more traditional neck bones in gamjatang can be a bit more difficult to source, not to mention they take a little longer to cook. Third, nothing against barbecue, but if you've never had spare ribs stewed in a spicy broth until meltingly yielding, then you simply haven't lived.

Regardless of what kind of pork bones you end up using, this dish is, according to my mother, all about the meat. You want wonderfully tender pork to pick up with your fingers and gnaw at between spoonfuls of the fragrant, perilla-scented broth. For us, ribs fit that bill (and frankly, are easier to eat). Anyway, there's always the other gamja: Korean yellow potatoes, which are dreamily fluffy. If you don't live near a Korean grocery store that stocks these lovely spuds, then you can use Yukon Gold in a pinch.

2 pounds pork spare ribs on the rack, cut into 2 to 3 slabs (depending on the size of your pot)

6 heads baby bok choy (about 1½ pounds total), root ends cut off and leaves separated

3 large Korean yellow potatoes (about 1 pound), peeled and cut into 1-inch-thick slices

2-inch piece fresh ginger, finely grated

¼ cup soup soy sauce (see page 23)

¼ cup gochugaru

3 tablespoons gochujang

2 tablespoons doenjang (see page 23)

2 tablespoons maesil cheong (green plum syrup; see page 22)

1 teaspoon sugar

7 large garlic cloves, finely grated

½ medium yellow onion, thinly sliced

20 large fresh perilla leaves

1 large jalapeño, seeded and thinly sliced into rings (optional)

Cooked white rice (page 128), for serving

SERVES 4 TO 6

1. In a large pot, combine the spare ribs, bok choy, and water to cover. Bring to a boil over high heat and cook for 5 minutes (this step is just to get rid of any scum from the pork, but also to tamp down some of its gaminess, as well as to cook the vegetables). Drain and set aside the bok choy for later.

2. Return the ribs to the pot and cover with water. Bring to a boil over high heat. Reduce the heat to medium-low and gently boil until the ribs are tender (they should fall off the bone easily but still have some juiciness and chew), 40 to 50 minutes.

3. Add the potatoes and continue cooking until a fork slides in and out of the spuds easily, about 20 more minutes.

4. Meanwhile, in a medium bowl, stir together the ginger, soy sauce, gochugaru, gochujang, doenjang, plum syrup, sugar, and garlic and add the reserved bok choy, tossing to combine.

5. When the potatoes are done, add the seasoned bok choy to the pot, along with the onion, perilla leaves, and optional jalapeño. Bring the heat up to high so the soup boils rapidly, and cook until the onion and perilla leaves have just lost their raw edge (the perilla will also reduce significantly in the heat, sort of like spinach), about 5 minutes.

6. Serve with white rice.

Seolleongtang Noodles
with Scallion Gremolata

This is one of my favorite Korean restaurant dishes: the milkiest ox bone soup, gentle and savory, with soft nests of wheat-flour noodles resting at the bottom of the bowl and a shower of raw scallions and garlic floating on top. But there was a point, living in New York City, when I saw the price of this dish increase. It used to cost less than $10 for a bowl, now it's nearly double; not only that, but the soup at these restaurants has also become more and more diluted with water. Nothing is more depressing than watching your favorite childhood foods become too expensive for you to eat (except for perhaps watching them become diluted, too). Which is why this is one of those dishes that is absolutely worth making yourself at home, not least because when you cook this yourself, you can double the noodle amount. The noodles were always my favorite part anyway, and my bowl never seemed to have enough. A true seolleongtang is about the milky broth, to be sure, and the somyeon noodles are secondary. But I'm an adult now, so let's stop dilly-dallying: My version is a noodle dish. Even with the increased carbohydrates here, I still like to eat this with white rice like you would at a restaurant (because I would never say no to a little double-carb action).

The bones are an initial investment, yes, but you'll see that you can get at least two to three more uses out of them (see Note on page 118). And anyway, the soup will become whiter and whiter, milkier and milkier, the more you use the bones. (It's the marrow, in case you were wondering.) You'll be surprised at how many tries it takes to truly deplete them of their milky store. As Jean told me years ago over the phone, it takes time for the bones to let off their goodness. This is the kind of thing you'll want to cook on a long weekend, when you have the three hours required to really let the bone broth go.

I do find that a quick last-minute gremolata, made simply by tossing a handful of ingredients together, helps to brighten things up and entice the belly. You can use whatever fresh herbs you like, but in homage to the original seolleongtang, I call for thinly sliced scallions for vegetal heft, grated raw garlic for mild heat, and a sprinkle of flaky sea salt (the crunchy kind) for texture and pops of saline. It sounds fussier than it is, but don't skip it. It makes a huge difference in the eating experience and tastes wonderful.

RECIPE CONTINUES

5 pounds beef bones (especially marrow, leg, tail, shin, stuff like that; see Note)

1 pound brisket

1 large yellow onion, halved

2 large scallions, thinly sliced on the diagonal

2 large garlic cloves, finely grated

1 teaspoon flaky sea salt

Freshly ground black pepper

8 ounces somyeon (thin wheat noodles), cooked according to package instructions, rinsed, and drained

Cooked white rice (page 128), for serving

Seolleongtang-Restaurant Radish Kimchi (optional; page 74), for serving

SERVES 4 TO 6

1. In the biggest pot you've got, add the beef bones and brisket and cover by 2 inches with cold tap water. Bring to a boil over high heat and cook for 10 minutes so the impurities from the bones rise to the surface of the water. Drain, discarding the cooking liquid, and rinse the bones in the sink. Return them to the pot, cover by 2 inches with more cold tap water, add the onion, and set over high heat. Bring to a boil, then reduce the heat to medium-low, loosely cover with a lid, and cook at a gentle boil until the stock is rich and milky, 3 to 3½ hours. (You can add more water if the liquid reduces too much—you want there to be 4 to 6 cups of broth in the pot.)

2. In the last few minutes of cooking, in a small bowl, mix together the scallions, garlic, and flaky sea salt. Season with black pepper and set aside.

3. When the stock is rich and milky, strain it in a colander set over a large bowl. Take the brisket out and let it cool slightly until it's easier to handle; when it's manageable, slice it thinly against the grain, and return it to the empty pot. Discard the onion and scallions. If there's any meat or yummy cartilage clinging to the beef bones, remove it and place it in the pot as well (or enjoy as a chef's treat). Cool the bones and then freeze them in a plastic bag to use another time; they can be reused another two or three times (see Note).

4. Pour the stock back into the pot with the brisket meat and trimmings. Bring to a boil over high heat and, using a ladle, skim any excess fat if you'd like.

5. Divide the somyeon noodles among the bowls and top with the hot broth. Serve with white rice, radish kimchi (if using), and the scallion gremolata on the side, to be sprinkled over the noodles as desired.

Note Though you could use any marrow-rich beef bone, you'll be able to find these specific sagol (from the knuckles, feet, and shin, all great for a rich, milky seolleongtang) in the freezer section of Korean and other Asian supermarkets, often labeled "beef bones."

Mountain Kalbitang with
All of the Herbs page 120

Mountain Kalbitang
with All of the Herbs

Jean makes kimchi fried rice whenever I come home, but she makes kalbitang, an aromatic beef short rib soup, whenever my big brother Kevin comes home. It's his favorite Korean dish. "I love that over time it gets more flavorful," he wrote to me in a text message once. "The meat becomes softer, more fall-off-the-bone, the radish slices soak up the broth and start breaking apart, and the spring onions become sweeter." One spring, in Korea, when my dad took Kevin to visit my grandmother's grave in the mountains, they went to a kalbitang restaurant afterward. As Kevin tells it, it was a homey restaurant with an old lady in the back making the soup. "It felt like Grandma herself was feeding us," he said.

Unlike some of the other punchier soups and stews in this chapter, this one—my brother's desert-island dish—is mild and mellow, but in the best ways. And it really is greater than the sum of its parts. You start with hardly any meat, but the broth is fortified with umami-rich ingredients like onions, garlic, and dasima (dried kelp, which has an incredibly high quotient of glutamate, the thing that makes our tongues perceive umami), all of which results in a clean but savory soup. I love that the predominant flavoring here is Korean radish, which is sweet and vegetal—and once boiled for hours, gets tender-bellied and imbued with beefy flavor.

My recipe admittedly has less broth than traditional versions of this dish, but that's because I cook it way down to produce a rich soup. Liquid gold, like alchemy. It feels quite springlike, too, with all the herbs, which add brightness and additional flavor at the end. If you're not a fan of parsley and mint—or if you're a purist—feel free to leave them out. But I love how they add to the freshness of the final dish, a soup of the mountains, where Grandma lives.

2 pounds English-cut bone-in beef short ribs (frozen ribs are okay)

1 large yellow onion, halved

7 large garlic cloves, smashed with the side of a knife

2 daepa or 4 scallions, thinly sliced on the diagonal

1 (5-inch) square dasima (dried kelp; see page 23)

½ pound Korean radish, peeled and cut crosswise into 1-inch steaks

1 teaspoon kosher salt, plus more as needed

1 teaspoon soup soy sauce (see page 23), plus more as needed

Freshly ground black pepper

Fresh mint leaves and cilantro leaves with tender stems, for garnish

SERVES 2

1. Soak the ribs in a bowl of cold water for 30 minutes. (I often start from frozen short ribs anyway, so this step is also how I simultaneously thaw them.)

2. After soaking, drain the ribs and add them to a large soup pot with the onion, garlic, half of the daepa, the dasima, radish, salt, and 10 cups water. Bring to a boil over high heat. Reduce the heat to medium-low, loosely cover with a lid, and cook at a gentle boil until the ribs are tender and seem about to fall off the bone, 2 to 2½ hours. Carefully remove the ribs (and meat) and radish steaks and set aside.

3. Strain the stock through a colander into a large bowl or measuring cup (you should have 7 to 8 cups of broth). Discard the solids. Skim off any fat, if you'd like, and discard. Return the stock to the same pot and add the ribs and radish steaks. Bring to a boil. Cook for 5 more minutes. Turn off the heat and taste for seasoning; add the soup soy sauce, black pepper to taste, and more salt if needed.

4. Serve in large bowls and garnish with the remaining daepa and herbs.

Kalbijjim
with Root Vegetables and Beef-Fat Croutons

Kalbijjim is the ultimate Korean braised dish—but the braise in question involves gently boiling short ribs until they're fall-apart tender, then finishing them in a sweet and salty dream of a soy sauce broth. Balanced by brown sugar, maple syrup, and a little grated apple, this is a redolent braise with great popular appeal, the beef stew recipe everyone likes.

Growing up, I only ever had it at birthdays and fancy parties, so learning how to make it as an adult felt like a real rite of passage. It does take a couple days to make, however, as you'll want to refrigerate the beef stock to remove the fat, and then use that fat to fry up some croutons in the oven (which is why I would start this the night before you plan to eat it). Kalbijjim is not an everyday food, to be sure; it's a special occasion. But who's to say dinner can't be a special occasion?

2 pounds English-cut bone-in beef short ribs (frozen ribs are okay)

½ large yellow onion, halved

2 large jalapeños, thickly sliced crosswise

7 large garlic cloves, smashed with the side of a knife

2-inch piece fresh ginger, thickly sliced

½ small red apple

5 tablespoons soy sauce

2 tablespoons dark brown sugar

2 tablespoons maple syrup

4 large red radishes, halved

1 large carrot, thickly sliced on the diagonal

2 daepa or 4 large scallions, thinly sliced

½ pound chewy bread, such as country-style sourdough, crusts removed and torn into bite-size pieces (about 2 cups)

Pinch of kosher salt

Cooked white rice (page 128), for serving

SERVES 4

1. Soak the ribs in a bowl of cold water for 30 minutes.

2. Drain and add the ribs to a large soup pot with the onion, half of the jalapeños, the garlic, ginger, and 8 cups cold tap water. Bring to a boil over high heat. Reduce the heat to medium, partially cover with a lid, and continue gently boiling until the ribs are tender and the stock is reduced by three-quarters, about 1 hour 30 minutes. You should be left with about 2 cups stock, including fat. If you have more, then keep boiling and reducing; if you have less, then add water.

3. Remove the ribs from the pot and set aside. Drain the stock through a sieve into a bowl, discarding the solids. Cover the bowl with plastic and refrigerate overnight. Cover and refrigerate the cooked short ribs, as well.

4. The next day, use a fork to remove the solidified fat from the surface of the stock and transfer it to a small microwave-safe bowl.

5. Meanwhile, grate the apple into a small bowl and stir in the soy sauce, brown sugar, and maple syrup.

6. Place the ribs in a large pot. Pour in the reserved beef stock and apple-soy mixture and bring to a boil over high heat. Reduce the heat to medium and continue gently boiling until the stock has reduced by about half, 10 to 15 minutes. Add the remaining jalapeño, the radishes, carrot, and half of the daepa and continue boiling until the vegetables have softened, about 15 minutes.

7. Meanwhile, to make the croutons, preheat the oven to 400°F.

8. If the beef fat is still hard, microwave in 10-second intervals to melt. On a sheet pan, toss the bread pieces with the melted beef fat, the remaining scallions, and salt. Bake until the bread is crispy, about 10 minutes.

9. Serve the kalbijjim with the scallion-y beef-fat croutons scattered atop each serving and some white rice.

Rice Cuisine

Jipbap means "home food"

Bap meogeosseo? Denotatively, this translates to "Did you eat rice?" But when you say that in a Korean household, what you really mean connotatively is: How are you? Did you eat yet? Let me warm up a bowl for you. My grandma's version of this was: "Want me to fry you an egg?" By the time I was old enough to answer such a question, she was too old and couldn't cook anymore. She would apologize for it all the time. But the one thing she could do, despite her arthritis, was fry a deliciously runny sunny-side up egg. And once she fried that egg, we were already halfway to dinner since the rice cooker was perpetually brimming with sticky white rice.

Rice is the bedrock of Korean home cooking. It's baked into the language: Jipbap is food you eat at home (*jip* referring to "home" and *bap* referring to "food," though literally it also translates to "rice"). In a cultural context like Korean cuisine, where steamed rice is served with nearly every meal—among a sea of banchan, maybe with a stew or a grilled meat—it makes sense that the word for cooked rice, bap, would also be a homonym for the word for food. Because in Korea, food means rice, and rice means food. And jipbap means home food.

Whenever I'm cooking, my psyche will wander, and wherever it lands, I can rest assured that it always has a landing pad of freshly steamed white rice. And not without reason: The bland, comforting canvas of white rice is the perfect counterpoint to saucier, more boldly flavored dishes like glazed proteins and brothy stews. I call for rice not because I hate noodles or bread, or because I'm Asian; I call for it because it tastes good. "Rice dishes, whether sweet, spicy, hot, cold, oniony, salty, or creamy, are the go-to food for many of us when we seek comfort," writes the wonderful food writer and culinary historian Michael W. Twitty in his book *Rice*. "For many of us southerners, no other ingredient tastes this much like home."

Depending on where you are in the world, how you grew up, and who loved you, rice means something different to you. I love this chapter because it's a collection of some of the most comforting Korean American home cooking in the world, like the Spam and Perilla Kimbap (page 138), the Sheet-Pan Bibimbap with Roasted Fall

Vegetables (page 150), and the Winter Squash Risotto with Chewy Rice Cakes (page 153). Many of the everyday recipes in this chapter serve one and can be doubled or quadrupled easily. But I wrote them like this because rice cuisine is food you make for yourself with the leftover white rice in the rice cooker, whether it's my Kimchi Fried Rice with Egg Yolk (page 136), a late-night pantry meal; Tomato-y Omelet Rice (page 133), ketchup fried rice that gets topped with a fluffy omelet; or Gyeranbap with Roasted Seaweed and Capers (page 130), a fried egg and soy sauce stirred into a bowl of rice. These recipes are comforting to cook because they're all fairly quick and simple (if you have rice, then you have dinner), but they're also doubly comforting to eat because rice is a carbohydrate. And carbohydrates taste good.

I've always respected the adaptability of rice. It's crossed continents and survived hardships, growing well and yielding a high crop anywhere there's water. Like my parents. They say you're either a noodle person or a rice person. To that, my dad said it best at dinner one night: "I could live without noodles, but I couldn't live without rice."

Perfect White Rice

My mother and I are both equally evangelical about rice—especially steamed white rice. But we differ greatly in how we wash it, only to meet again at the end in the rice cooker, like a fugue that finally homogenizes. Though I love the convenience of a rice cooker (and feel that everyone should own one), sometimes when I'm at an Airbnb or cooking at a friend's house, I like to make rice on the stovetop. It always reminds me of how good—and more complex—it can sometimes taste than the electric stuff. So here, I offer my stovetop method and Jean's rice cooker version, to cover all our bases.

Depending on what kind of cook you are—an Eric or a Jean—here are two methods of arriving at the very subjective title of "Perfect White Rice." Perfect to whom? To me, perfect means soft, fluffy grains, light as clouds, but not mushy or hard. Just right. To my mother, same (she just doesn't measure anything). But I still believe that if something else is perfect to *you*, then that's perfect, too. So adjust the water according to what you like. These are mine and Jean's proportions, and they're a good place to start, as you'll be making lots of rice while cooking through this book.

And if you need to make more than the three cups here, then just double or triple the recipe according to your needs. The main rule of thumb when steaming short- or medium-grain white rice is that you're going for a 1:1 ratio of rice to water, which is perfect as long as you're not skipping the soaking step, which helps the grains cook more evenly.

Eric's "Perfect White Rice" (Stovetop Method)

1 cup medium-grain white rice, such as Calrose

1 cup water

MAKES 3 CUPS COOKED RICE

1. Place the rice in a sieve and hold it under cold, running water, shaking it often, until the water runs clear.

2. Place the rinsed rice and 1 cup water into a small pot and let the rice soak for 10 minutes.

3. Set the pot over high heat and let the water come to a simmer, then reduce the heat to low, cover the pot, and continue simmering for 20 minutes. After 20 minutes, remove from the heat and let it sit, still covered, for 10 minutes to steam and get fluffy. (Don't peek, as much of the cooking happens in this resting stage.) Fluff with a fork before serving.

RECIPE CONTINUES

Jean's "Perfect White Rice" (Rice Cooker Method)

1 coffee mugful of medium-grain white rice, such as Calrose

Water

MAKES 3 CUPS COOKED RICE

1. Place the rice in the bowl insert of a rice cooker and run it under the cold tap. Swish your hand around the rice and water, occasionally rubbing the grains between your fingers. Change out the water three to four times, carefully pouring it out the edge of the bowl, making sure not to lose any of the grains by keeping your other hand under the stream of cloudy rice water.

2. In the now mostly drained (but still pretty wet) rice, add enough water so that when you press your hand flat over the rice it reaches the first crease on your wrist. This is, of course, assuming your rice cooker insert is big enough and your hand small enough (mine never are, which is why I measure this; also, science). Let the rice soak for 10 minutes to an hour.

3. Place the rice cooker insert into the rice cooker and turn it on. As soon as it finishes steaming, fluff the rice with a flat plastic rice spoon to prevent clumping later.

Gyeranbap
with Roasted Seaweed and Capers

I love the ubiquity of gyeranbap: If you're Korean, then it's likely you already know that mixing fried eggs, soy sauce, and sesame oil into a bowl of white rice tastes bomb. It makes sense that these four basic pantry staples would coalesce into a timeless dish that we eat because our parents ate it, who ate it because their parents ate it, and so on. Also, it's just so easy: This is the kind of food you make for yourself when you're hungry but too tired to cook—and perhaps you're on your own for the evening, so you don't want to spend too much time in the kitchen.

There are many ways to a good gyeranbap, but my method has been carefully perfected over the years: I like to fry my eggs in the soy sauce and sesame oil you would ordinarily drizzle atop at the end. This way, the sesame oil can act as both cooking fat and seasoning for the rice, and the soy sauce can reduce slightly and lose some of its raw edge, caramelizing around the lacy edges of the fried egg. The result? A darn good gyeranbap.

1 cup cooked white rice
  (page 128), preferably fresh

2 teaspoons toasted sesame oil

¾ teaspoon soy sauce, plus
  more to taste

2 large eggs

1 (5-gram) packet gim, crushed
  with your hands

Capers, for serving

Freshly ground black pepper

SERVES 1

1. Add the rice to a medium bowl and set aside.

2. In a medium nonstick skillet, heat the sesame oil and soy sauce over high heat. Crack in the eggs. Reduce the heat if the splatter is too much, but otherwise just cook until the whites have pillowed up, slightly crisped around the edges, and the white area around the yolk is no longer liquidy, about 1 minute (if your pan is hot enough; longer if it isn't). Also, the soy sauce should have stained the whites and bubbled up, turning into a sticky glaze.

3. Slide the fried eggs over the rice, shower with the gim, and dot with a few capers. Season with pepper. Mix everything together with a spoon before tasting. This is where you can adjust for seasoning, adding more soy sauce as needed.

Tomato-y Omelet Rice

Omurice—a fried rice dish topped with an omelet that gets zigzagged with ketchup—is a mainstay at Korean bunsik restaurants, which are restaurants that serve "snack" items like kimbap, tteokbokki, and ramyun. When cooking this dish at home, sometimes the omelet doesn't turn out perfect, and that's okay. The important thing to note is that whatever shape your eggs take, they will be soft-bellied and seasoned *just* right. And that's the real point: the balance between the salty fried rice and the sweet, fluffy eggs—and, of course, the ketchup, which lends that comforting tomato flavor. I've found, too, that adding halved grape tomatoes to the fried rice juices up the tomato factor by a hundred, adding nice bursts of texture.

FOR THE FRIED RICE

1 tablespoon unsalted butter

½ medium yellow onion, diced

4 ounces grape tomatoes, halved (about ¾ cup)

2 scallions, thinly sliced on the diagonal

1 cup cooked white rice (page 128), fresh, day-old, or cold

1 teaspoon soy sauce

2 tablespoons ketchup, plus more for squirting on top

FOR THE OMELET

2 large eggs

¼ teaspoon kosher salt

¼ teaspoon sugar

Freshly ground black pepper

1 tablespoon unsalted butter

SERVES 1

1. Make the fried rice: In a large nonstick skillet, melt the butter over medium-high heat. Add the onion and cook, stirring constantly, until the onion just starts to soften (but is still crunchy), about 2 minutes. Add the grape tomatoes and continue stir-frying until warmed through, about 30 seconds.

2. Add the scallions and rice, drizzle with the soy sauce, and add the ketchup. Stir together to combine and fry the rice until aromatic, about 2 minutes. Taste and adjust for seasoning with salt.

3. Reduce the heat to low and let the rice crisp for 5 minutes. Transfer to a plate and set aside.

4. Make the omelet: Wipe out the skillet with a paper towel and set over medium-low heat. Crack the eggs into a bowl and whisk together with a splash of water, the salt, sugar, and pepper to taste. Melt the butter in the pan. Add the eggs and shake the pan vigorously with one hand while using a silicone spatula to jostle it, disturb it, and almost whisk it for 30 to 45 seconds. Reduce the heat to low and let the eggs set gently—without touching—for 2 to 3 minutes. Using the edge of your spatula, start to fold over one side, like you're wrapping a sleeping bag, until you get to the end and can roll the omelet out of the pan and onto the fried rice, seam-side down.

5. Squeeze some more ketchup over the omelet (make any design you wish) and serve immediately.

Nest

In 1973, the American literary critic Harold Bloom wrote about the "anxiety of influence" that contemporary poets have regarding their predecessors. The idea being that: Even though you want to place yourself within a genealogy by honoring the writers that came before you, there's an incredible weighted blanket of anxiety that stems from having to tread that tightrope between drawing inspiration from your heroes and iterating without originality.

That's how I feel about my mother and her cooking. Developing my own kimchi fried rice recipe, then, felt essential if I was to eventually break free from this anxiety I harbor of not living up to her legacy and her expertise as a Korean cook, but also of wanting to find my own voice in the kitchen. So instead of perfecting or replicating her Spam and fried egg–laden kimchi fried rice in this book, I've penned my own: a vegetarian version (not for any particular reason other than that the kimchi shines here, which I love). This one is much hotter, much spicier, much *redder* (thanks to an extra splash of kimchi juice and an aromatic tangle of hot butter, scallions, and gochugaru); and absolutely showered with onyx-black gim (that deeply savory roasted seaweed dream), which creates a little nest for one raw egg yolk in place of the fried egg. I believe this egg yolk is the best way to coat every single grain with golden velvet.

It doesn't taste like home. "It tastes like restaurant food," my dad told me when he ate this. My dish reminded him of the kimchi fried rice that waiters at Korean barbecue restaurants might prepare in front of you using the rendered fat and crispy flavor bits stuck to the grill pan after a meal of fatty, luscious samgyeopsal, or pork belly. It does taste like that. It also tastes like all the many plates of fiery, gochugaru-threaded kimchi fried rice I ate as a kid at the Korean restaurants along Buford Highway in Atlanta. It tastes, too, like those late-night bites my parents hid from us, not on purpose but because, in their words, "Oh, you kids wouldn't like this": fresh kimchi bibimbap, a makeshift product of midnight fridge raids, where they'd take various namul (seasoned vegetable) banchan and some kimchi, mix it all up, and head to bed to eat in front of the television.

This is not my mother's kimchi fried rice, which is comfortingly sweet and mellow. This is mine, and it tastes comforting in a different way, in the way that one might feel when finally leaving the nest.

Eric's Kimchi Fried Rice
with Egg Yolk

It helps with fried rice dishes to have a mise en place: meaning to have prepped and measured out all the ingredients before you start cooking. Because once you start, it all comes together very quickly. The one thing you don't want to do is burn the gochugaru or the kimchi, which is how you lose the bright red flavor that's characteristic of kimchi fried rice. I actually like the taste of the raw kimchi juice and all its red-peppery glory here; it's what makes this dish taste, as my dad said, "like fire."

1 tablespoon unsalted butter

1 large scallion, thinly sliced on the diagonal

½ teaspoon gochugaru (less if you don't like spicy)

½ medium yellow onion, diced

1 cup finely chopped, very ripe (like, the dankest you've got) napa cabbage kimchi, store-bought or homemade (page 68)

1 cup cooked white rice (page 128), fresh, day-old, or cold

2 tablespoons kimchi juice

1 teaspoon toasted sesame oil

½ teaspoon fish sauce

1 (5-gram) packet gim, crushed with your hands

1 large raw egg yolk (one you feel confident about)

SERVES 1

1. In a large nonstick or cast-iron skillet, melt the butter over medium-low heat. Add the scallion and gochugaru and sauté for 30 seconds to bloom the chile flakes.

2. Still over medium-low, add the onion and sauté until just beginning to sweat, about 1 minute. Stir in the kimchi and sauté for another minute. Place the rice in a mound in the center of the pan, over the other ingredients, and drizzle it with the kimchi juice, sesame oil, and fish sauce. Then stir the rice and kimchi together and cook over high heat for 3 minutes. Using the back of your spoon, gently press the rice into the pan (like you're making a big kimchi fried rice pancake); reduce the heat to medium and let the rice crisp for 2 minutes.

3. Serve in a bowl topped with the gim (I like to shape it into a nest) and egg yolk, which should be placed ever so gently within the gim nest. To eat, stir the egg yolk into the hot rice.

Spam and Perilla Kimbap page 138

Spam and Perilla Kimbap

In 2015, lost and unemployed, I had just dropped out of my PhD program in literature and had never been more depressed. Those were some of the darkest months of my life. One light at the end of the tunnel was a sushi lunch I had with a former boss of mine at Food Network, Michelle Buffardi. She wanted to meet because she had a potential job for me, if I wanted it. I didn't even know if I wanted it, but I knew that I trusted her, so I took it. Taking that job was the best decision I've ever made because it led to my career in food media, which led to me becoming a writer, which led to this book you're holding now in your hands.

I remember every detail of that day. What I was wearing, how lost I felt, and how grateful I was for the lunch that I was sharing with this wonderful woman who's meant so much to me over the years. One particular roll we ate at that meal had a bitter, nutty herb punctuating the crispy, fatty other bits. This kimbap is an homage to that pivotal moment, when I suddenly started to feel the ground under my feet again, sparked by the seaweed-wrapped kindness that helped me, as they say, find the light.

Kimbap isn't hard to make, but it does require a little math. Luckily, I've done all of it for you: One of the most satisfying things in life, you'll find, too, is using up every last bit of the filling and rice and ending up with four perfect rolls. These are wonderful in a packed lunch or even at a picnic, not least because they travel beautifully. Be sure to get the unsalted, unroasted gim meant for kimbap (not the salted, roasted kind for snacking). It's often labeled as "dried laver" at Korean grocery stores. If you don't want Spam, then I'd go with another filling, like the Cheeseburger Kimbap (page 141).

2 cups cooked white rice (page 128), fresh or day-old

1 tablespoon plus 1 teaspoon toasted sesame oil, plus more for greasing a plate

Kosher salt

6 ounces Spam (half a 12-ounce can), sliced lengthwise into eight 3½ × ¾ × ¾-inch sticks

¼ teaspoon garlic powder

1 tablespoon maple syrup

4 (7½ × 8-inch) sheets unseasoned kimbap gim

24 fresh perilla leaves

SERVES 4

1. In a medium bowl, add the rice and 1 tablespoon of the sesame oil, season with salt, and gently stir together with a plastic rice scooper or rubber spatula (to minimize sticking). You'll notice the grains start to glisten and separate thanks to the nutty sesame oil. Set the seasoned rice aside to cool if it's not already.

2. Grease a plate with a little sesame oil. Set a large, cold nonstick skillet on the stove, turn the heat to medium-high, and add the remaining 1 teaspoon sesame oil and the Spam, frying until caramelized at the edges, 3 to 4 minutes. Add the garlic powder and maple syrup, toss with the Spam pieces, and cook the syrup down, tossing and turning the Spam occasionally, until the syrup reduces and glazes the outsides with shiny amber and even some darker caramelized bits, about 1 minute. Set aside on the greased plate.

3. Lay one sheet of kimbap gim, shiny-side up, on a cutting board or clean counter in front of you, a shorter side closest to you. Spread ½ cup of the seasoned rice as evenly as you can across the entire surface area of the gim. (A plastic rice scooper is best for this—again, the sticking—but you can use any implement you like, keeping a small bowl of water nearby to wet your hands if things get sticky.)

4. About one-third up from the bottom, lay 6 perilla leaves (two stacks of 3) over the rice and top with 2 pieces of maple-candied Spam laterally across the perilla, creating a straight pink line (see the photo on page 137).

5. Starting from the bottom, tightly roll the kimbap like a sleeping bag or cinnamon roll. Once rolled, use both hands to gently squeeze the roll even tighter together, compacting the rice, gim, Spam, and perilla into each other, fusing as one. With a very sharp knife, cut ¾-inch-thick pieces. Repeat to make 3 more kimbaps.

6. These are at their best when eaten slightly warm, but also taste great at room temperature.

Cheeseburger Kimbap (opposite) and
Spam and Perilla Kimbap (page 138)

Cheeseburger Kimbap

If Spam's not your thing, then this invention from my thirteen-year-old self might do it for you: kimbap with all the flavors of a classic cheeseburger. Though you need the cheese and burger for this to be a cheeseburger kimbap proper, the true key to that nostalgic taste exists, for me, within the mayochup (mayonnaise and ketchup), raw onion (trust me), and pickle (lots of it).

1 cup cooked white rice (page 128), fresh or day-old

2 teaspoons toasted sesame oil

Kosher salt

2 tablespoons unsalted butter

8 ounces ground beef

½ teaspoon garlic powder

Freshly ground black pepper

¼ cup finely diced yellow onion

2 tablespoons chopped kosher dill pickles, plus 1 to 2 pickles, quartered lengthwise

1 tablespoon mayonnaise

2 tablespoons ketchup

2 (7½ × 8-inch) sheets unseasoned kimbap gim

2 slices American cheese, halved

SERVES 2

1. In a medium bowl, stir together the rice and sesame oil, season with salt, and gently stir everything together with a plastic rice scooper or rubber spatula (to minimize sticking) until evenly combined. You'll notice the grains start to glisten and separate thanks to the nutty sesame oil. Set the seasoned rice aside to cool if it's not already.

2. In a large skillet, melt the butter over medium-high heat. Add the ground beef and garlic powder and season with salt and pepper. Fry, stirring occasionally, until browned, evenly caramelized and crispy at the edges, and no longer pink, about 8 minutes. Drain off the fat and transfer the beef to a medium bowl. Add the onion, chopped pickles, mayonnaise, and ketchup to the beef and stir until well combined.

3. Lay one sheet of kimbap gim, shiny-side up, on a cutting board or clean counter in front of you, a shorter side facing you. Spread ½ cup of the seasoned rice as evenly as you can across the entire surface area of the seaweed. (A plastic rice scooper is best for this—again, the sticking—but you can use any implement you like, keeping a small bowl of water nearby to wet your hands if things get sticky.)

4. About one-third up from the bottom, lay two American cheese halves (they should be long rectangles) end to end over the rice, creating a straight orange line across the width of the surface. Spoon the beef laterally across the cheese, creating a straight, fairly contained line. Finally, place the quartered pickles, as many as you like, over the beef.

5. Starting from the bottom, tightly roll the kimbap like a sleeping bag or cinnamon roll. Once rolled, use both hands to gently squeeze the roll even tighter together, compacting the rice, seaweed, hamburger filling, and American cheese into each other, fusing as one. With a very sharp knife, cut crosswise into ¾-inch-thick pieces. Repeat to make 1 more kimbap.

6. These are at their best when eaten slightly warm, but also taste great at room temperature.

Summer Albap
with Perilla and Salted Garden Vegetables

This albap, a simple bowl of white rice dribbled with nutty sesame oil and dotted with various tints of flying fish roe, is a quick and lovely summer lunch for two. In fact, it's inspired by a dish my mom and I eat together often at a Korean-owned Japanese restaurant on Buford Highway called Kang Nam. The fish roe is key here, not because it's beautiful (though of course it is), but because it's the main seasoning in this dish, adding umami-rich pops of saline throughout the rice. Do look for the jewel-bright colored flying fish roe, because each has its own flavor: For instance, the green roe tastes like wasabi, the black one squid ink, the red is colored with beets, the yellow with yuzu, and so on. However, the more easily found regular orange flying fish roe works well, too.

I like to describe my take on albap as a salad in rice form—and because I'm using red tomatoes, green cukes, and zucchini from my mother's garden, I often stick to that color palette and use red and green fish roe (but you can use whatever's available to you). All this dish requires is a little knife work and about 10 minutes to let the vegetables marinate in salt and vinegar. As you're building your albap, you may feel inspired to top it with other vegetables you prefer more or have on hand. I've tried this with raw corn, roasted eggplant, and even blanched summer green beans. The "salad" part is really just a blank canvas for the real star: the roe and the rice. This is especially great with the Maeuntang on page 169.

1 cup halved cherry tomatoes (about 5 ounces)

1 medium cucumber, diced (about 1 cup)

1 medium zucchini, diced (about 1 cup)

Kosher salt

¾ teaspoon sugar

3 teaspoons rice vinegar

2 cups freshly cooked white rice (page 128)

4 teaspoons toasted sesame oil

4 tablespoons flying fish roe (in various colors if possible)

18 fresh perilla leaves, rolled into a cigar shape and thinly sliced across into long strips

1 cup fresh cilantro leaves plus tender stems

SERVES 2

1. Place the tomatoes, cucumber, and zucchini in three separate small bowls. Season each with salt, ¼ teaspoon sugar, and 1 teaspoon vinegar and toss. Set aside to marinate for 10 minutes.

2. Divide the rice between two wide bowls. Top each bowl with 2 teaspoons sesame oil and 2 tablespoons fish roe. In small groupings over the rice, add the three marinated vegetables, the perilla, and cilantro.

3. To eat, just mix everything together and dive right in.

Sheet-Pan Bibimbap
with Roasted Fall Vegetables

I call this sheet-pan bibimbap because all of the cooking, from start to finish, happens on two 18 × 13-inch rimmed baking sheets. One main reason we never ate bibimbap growing up was because it always took too long and my mother didn't want to do all that work (understandably). Where ordinarily you would pan-fry each individual vegetable separately to maintain those satisfying color blocks, then make an omelet and slice it, and even marinate some bulgogi for the meat component should you be going that route, roasting everything on a sheet pan means you can just set it and forget it. It's bibimbap for the patient but lazy.

The other bibimbap recipes in this book prove that bibimbap is, at its core, a fridge-raid meal. It's what happens when you have remnants of leftover banchan lingering in the fridge and just throw them all in a bowl with some leftover white rice, sesame oil, and gochujang. It's supposed to be chill. In my version here, roasting all your vegetables on a sheet pan means you can arrive at bibimbap without standing over a stove, sautéing each ingredient individually. It's also a really satisfying way to get as many different vegetables into one dish as possible (or to clean out your crisper drawer before the next grocery run). Even more, the vegetables will be caramelized and even charred at the edges, making this recipe a hearty fall meal. Then it's just a matter of calling the family down for dinner to assemble their own bowls straight from the sheet pans.

This is my homage to fall, but you can use whatever vegetables you like. The butternut squash is key, though, in my opinion, especially once roasted until crispy-edged like honeyed chips. Their sweetness is doubly wonderful against the tart, crunchy apple and the mushrooms. The kale chips add a little salty something, though sautéed spinach is more traditional. Even Jean loves this sheet-pan method, saying it's the reason she now makes bibimbap for herself whenever she's craving vegetables.

RECIPE CONTINUES

1 pound butternut squash
(don't bother peeling it),
seeded and cut into bite-size
pieces (about 4 cups)

Olive oil

Kosher salt and freshly ground
black pepper

10 ounces wild mushrooms,
especially shiitake (stems
removed) and oyster, torn
into bite-size pieces
(about 3 cups)

1 medium red onion, halved and
thinly sliced

1 large red apple, halved, cored,
and cut into bite-size pieces

4 ounces Tuscan (lacinato) kale,
chopped into 1-inch pieces
(about 4 cups)

4 cups freshly cooked white rice
(page 128)

2 teaspoons toasted sesame oil

4 teaspoons gochujang

4 large raw egg yolks (ones you
feel confident about)

SERVES 4

1. Preheat the oven to 450°F.

2. On a sheet pan, toss the butternut squash with 2 tablespoons olive oil and season with salt and pepper. Slide to one half of the pan. Add the mushrooms and onions to the other half of the pan. Toss with 2 tablespoons olive oil and season with salt and pepper. Bake until the butternut squash and mushroom-onion mixture are crispy and burnished, about 45 minutes.

3. Meanwhile, on another sheet pan, arrange the apples and kale separately, one on each half of the pan. Toss each with 1 tablespoon olive oil and season with salt and pepper and set aside.

4. Once the squash and mushrooms have had their 45 minutes, take them out of the oven and toss them with a silicone spatula. Return the pan to the oven along with the second pan with the apples and kale. Bake until the kale has wilted slightly and become crispy, the apple slices are slightly softened, and the squash, onion, and mushrooms are even more caramelized, about 15 minutes.

5. Divide the rice evenly among four large bowls. To each bowl, add 1 teaspoon gochujang and ½ teaspoon sesame oil. Divide the roasted vegetables and apple evenly among the four bowls, keeping them in color-blocked sections. Finish each bowl with a single egg yolk.

6. To eat, just mix everything together and dig in.

Winter Squash Risotto
with Chewy Rice Cakes

Thick, chewy tteok, or rice cakes, make this dish. Just be sure to buy the long cylindrical ones (and not the already sliced ovals), because then you can chop them up yourself into thick 1-inch pieces that stay chewy as all hell.

One useful note on my risotto technique: I like to use either chicken or vegetable Better Than Bouillon for this, because then all you have to do is spoon a tablespoon or so of the aromatic gunge into the rice and periodically pour water from a recently boiled electric kettle (something more Americans should adopt from the Brits), adding more liquid only once the previous addition has been fully absorbed. As you splash in more and more water, the rice will plump up, hydrating and diluting the concentrated bouillon paste. No extra pot of simmering stock needed. But should you prefer the traditional method where you heat the stock separately in a pot on the side, keeping it at a gentle simmer and ladling it into the rice for thirty minutes straight, then be my guest.

As for the squash, I was inspired by hobakjuk, or pumpkin porridge, one of those rare dishes we only ate at really traditional Korean restaurants, or at that one sushi place on Buford Highway, or at Grandma Carol's house on Chuseok. And so it always felt like a stolen treat. Sparked by the taste memory of that comforting porridge, I decided to use hobakjuk as the mantecatura, the final stage in risotto cookery when a pat of butter gets vigorously stirred in at the end, loosening the creamy grains into a panel of liquid velvet.

I've tried this with canned pumpkin and it tasted fine. But when they're in season, there's nothing like fresh kabocha squash, which, once gently steamed in the microwave, becomes much easier to cut and is also the fastest, cleanest, safest way to cook hard-shelled gourds. Not to mention freshly steamed winter squash has that deep, aromatic nutty flavor that's hard to replicate—nor should you want to.

RECIPE CONTINUES

¾ pound cooked, peeled, and seeded kabocha squash (about 2 packed cups; see Note)

½ cup heavy cream

3 tablespoons unsalted butter

2 tablespoons olive oil

4 shallots, roughly chopped

2 celery ribs, roughly chopped

Kosher salt and freshly ground black pepper

1 cup Arborio rice

2 dried or fresh bay leaves

½ cup dry white wine or vermouth

2 teaspoons Better Than Bouillon vegetable or chicken base

12 ounces tteok (rice cakes), cut into 1-inch pieces

½ cup finely grated Parmesan cheese, plus more for serving

SERVES 4 TO 6

1. Add 4 cups of water to an electric kettle (or saucepan) and bring to a boil.

2. In a food processor, puree the cooked squash and heavy cream until smooth. Set aside.

3. Heat a large, wide-rimmed saucepan or Dutch oven over medium-high heat. Melt the butter and add the olive oil, then add the shallots and celery. Season the vegetables with salt and pepper and sauté them until the shallots are translucent, stirring often, 2 to 3 minutes. Add the rice and bay leaves and stir until each grain of rice is slicked with the shallot-y fat and the rice smells slightly toasted, about 1 minute. Splash in the wine or vermouth and stir vigorously, letting it bubble up until basically evaporated, 30 to 60 seconds. Reduce the heat to low.

4. Stir in the Better Than Bouillon base and, working ½ cup at a time, begin gradually adding the hot water from the recently boiled kettle, stirring the rice calmly but vigorously so as to release all of its wonderful starches (which will help make the risotto creamy later). Continue adding more water only once the previous addition has been absorbed completely by the rice, until your rice is cooked to your liking (at this stage, I like my grains with a slight bite in the middle, like al dente pasta). This process can take anywhere between 20 to 30 minutes, depending on your stove, your pot, your rice, your heat level, and the temperature of your water.

5. Finally, stir in the rice cakes, as well as the squash and cream puree you made earlier, which should loosen up the risotto nicely. Cook this over low heat, stirring constantly, until the rice cakes are tender but still chewy, and the squash-draped risotto is warmed through, 4 to 5 minutes. Remove the bay leaves. Stir in the Parmesan, taste for seasoning, and serve immediately on large plates with forks, offering more cheese on the side for guests who want it.

Note If you bought a whole kabocha squash, microwave it on high for 2 to 3 minutes until the skin becomes easier to slice through with your sharpest chef's knife. (Be careful!) Then chop it up into a couple pieces, remove the seeds, and place in a large microwave-safe bowl with 2 tablespoons of water. Microwave on high until the squash is soft and cooked through, 5 to 7 minutes. After cooking, scrape the soft flesh out with a spoon and discard the skin.

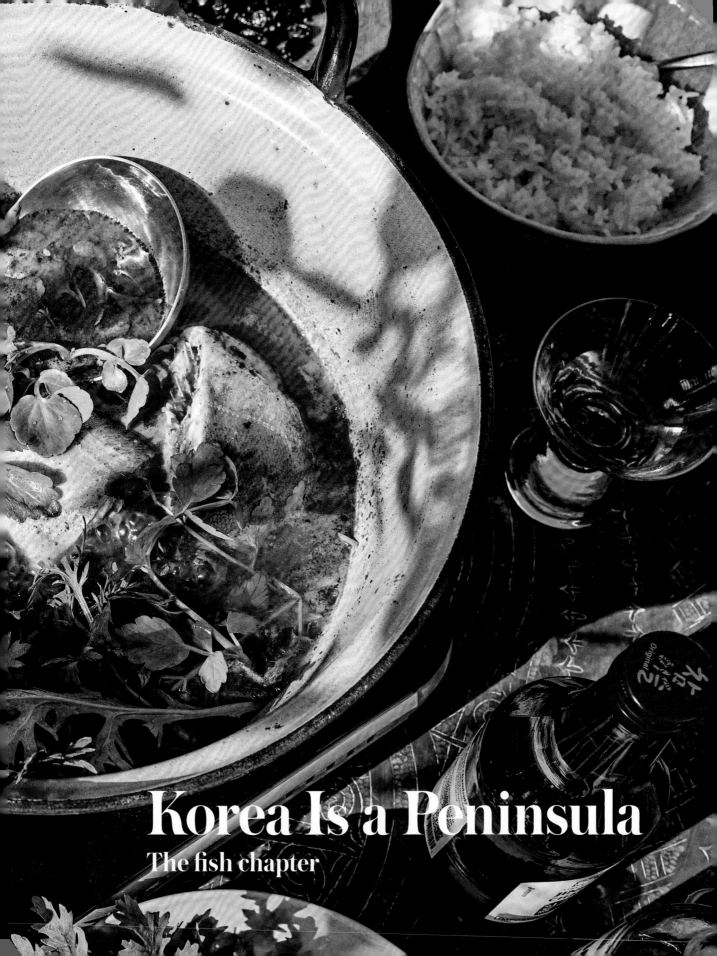

Korea Is a Peninsula

The fish chapter

When it comes to Korean home cooking, seafood deserves its own chapter.

It's a main ingredient, the meat to the potatoes (or more aptly, rice) of Korea, which makes sense because the country is surrounded by water on three sides. (Yes, Korea is a peninsula.) Growing up, we actually ate more fish than meat, in case that gives you an idea of how important these dishes are to my family. Mostly, I hope these preparations not only give you new ideas for what a fish dinner is and can be, but also teach you some basic techniques to apply to your own favorite cuts.

There's the Maeuntang (page 169), a spicy stew we made on fishing trips in North Carolina with flounder bones, though my version allows for fresh catch from a lake or river (or a grocery store). A simple sheet pan gets you toward the Salted Salmon Steaks with Celery and Mushrooms (page 165), which reiterates Jean's salting technique from the Pan-Fried Yellow Croaker (page 162), quite possibly our most regular protein in the house. The pièce de résistance is the Ganjang Gejang (page 176), raw soy sauce–marinated crabs, which are a Proustian madeleine for many Koreans. One bite of that nectarean crabmeat, rubbed into a bowl of fluffy white rice with a spoon, and you're home.

Jean, age twenty-something, cooking outdoors.

KOREAN AMERICAN

Salting Fish and Why It Rocks

We salt steaks in advance all the time—why not do the same with fish? The resultant flavor is just so much more deeply seasoned, not to mention the texture juicier, than if you were to simply salt it right before pan-frying. The one caveat with pan-frying fish at home, though, is the mess it makes of your kitchen. I won't pretend that's not a reality of eating delicious, crispy-skinned fish outside of a restaurant. Which is actually why, growing up, Jean cooked them outside on an electric George Foreman grill. The neighbors would stick their heads out, wondering what the smell was. "Oh, just frying some yellow croaker!" It's a fishy smell. Fried fish smells fishy. But unless you're eating an aromatic stew or a fresh, raw hoe platter on the spot (like, literally on the boat where you catch the fish), fishy fried fish also tastes really good. Especially the bone-in, skin-on stuff.

And it's not just croaker that tastes great salted. Any fatty bone-in, skin-on fish will do: a whole brook trout, for instance, or even a salmon steak. Once fried in some oil in a pan, the exteriors of salted fish get shatteringly crisp. It's a light dry brine, in essence. The salt isn't enough to turn the fish into jerky or lox—it just makes your supply last a little longer and taste a lot better. This practice stems from a history of preservation in Korea, back before refrigerators were a hot commodity. In fact, much of that preservation history (brining, fermenting, sun-drying, and salt-curing) is what makes Korean food what it is today: full of flavor and all about making what you have today keep until tomorrow.

Pan-Fried Yellow Croaker

When it comes to salted fish, yellow croaker is a good place to start. I used to take for granted this intensely fragrant (and delicious) whole fish my mom fried for us on weeknights. The way she would bring them home from the store after work, scale them in the sink (she never gutted them because the insides taste good; also: less work), and then shower them with crunchy salt. I remember opening the fridge to see the entire top shelf lined with these yellow-bellied beauts, stored in a wicker basket to air-dry and salt-cure, the critical step before frying the next day.

1 whole yellow croaker
  (about 10 ounces)
1 tablespoon coarse sea salt
Vegetable oil
Cooked white rice (page 128),
  for serving

SERVES 2

1. If your fishmonger hasn't already scaled your croaker for you, you'll want to do that now. In the sink, take a very sharp knife and use the sharp blade to carefully scrape it against the fish's skin until the scales start to come off. You may need to try a couple directions to find which way the scales run. Rinse under cold water and don't remove the insides unless you really want to.

2. Hold the croaker with one hand over the sink and generously sprinkle the entire surface (both sides of the fish and the head, too) with the salt. Though you don't really have to measure this (Jean never does), I'm offering measurements here because the ratio of salt to fish does matter. Whether you stray a little from these proportions *doesn't* matter, however, as long as it's seasoned enough for you. Place the salted fish in a basket or on a plate to dry out in the fridge overnight or for up to 72 hours.

3. When ready to fry, heat a large skillet or grill pan over medium-high heat. Add enough oil to generously coat the bottom of the pan and fry the fish until absolutely crispy and golden on both sides, 10 to 15 minutes total.

4. Serve with white rice.

Salted Salmon Steaks
with Celery and Mushrooms

Salmon steaks are much fattier than fillets, making them wonderful for roasting. Even better if you salt them ahead of cooking. Just thirty minutes of salting, like with a juicy cucumber, brings out the absolute best in fatty fish. What you're doing is concentrating the flavor and altering the texture of the proteins slightly to be firmer but juicier, full of briny wonder. I love the combination here of roasted mushrooms, which are wonderfully meaty, and thinly sliced celery, which stays fairly crunchy in the quick heat of the oven but also becomes even more like itself: aromatic and full of vegetal freshness.

Kosher salt and freshly ground black pepper

2 salmon steaks (about 6 ounces each)

2 celery stalks

8 ounces cremini mushrooms

2 tablespoons olive oil

Cooked white rice (page 128), for serving

SERVES 2

1. Generously salt and pepper the salmon steaks on both sides and place on a plate to dry-brine in the refrigerator for at least 30 minutes and up to 4 hours.

2. When ready to cook, preheat the oven to 450°F.

3. Remove the salmon from the fridge and let it warm to room temperature while the oven preheats and you prepare the vegetables: Thickly slice the celery on the diagonal and thinly slice the mushrooms. Transfer the vegetables to a sheet pan and drizzle with 1 tablespoon of the olive oil. Season the vegetables with salt and pepper and toss well, spreading into an even layer.

4. Nestle the salmon steaks in between the vegetables so the fish is touching the pan and there are no mushrooms or celery under either piece. Drizzle the remaining 1 tablespoon olive oil over both steaks, smearing it all over with your hands and flipping once or twice to evenly coat.

5. Roast until the salmon is cooked through (it should flake easily with a fork and look opaque inside) and the celery and mushrooms begin to caramelize at the edges, about 30 minutes.

6. Serve with white rice.

Crispy Trout
with White Wine and Lemon Butter

My Uncle Young used to take us trout fishing all the time in the mountains of North Carolina. After a day of fishing, he'd scale, gut, and fillet the catch for us and then batter them in flour and fry them up crisp. This dish is in honor of Uncle Young, a fisherman who loved driving and taking his nieces and nephews on long road trips to the Carolinas, and teaching us that fresh fish tastes best when prepared simply with a light sprinkling of salt and a spritz of lemon, always. You can find trout fillets at most grocery stores—filleting helps flatten the surface area, encouraging the skin to evenly crisp in the pan. I distinctly remember the taste of McCormick black pepper in this dish (you know, that ready-ground stuff that kind of tastes like white pepper). But if you don't have it, freshly ground is more than fine.

2 tablespoons all-purpose flour

2 skin-on trout fillets
(5 to 6 ounces each)

Kosher salt and ground black or
white pepper

Vegetable oil

½ cup dry white wine

2 tablespoons fresh lemon juice,
plus wedges for serving

2 tablespoons cold unsalted
butter

1 tablespoon capers

Fresh dill, for serving

Cooked white rice (page 128),
for serving

SERVES 2

1. Add the flour to a plate slightly larger than the size of the trout fillets. Season the trout fillets with salt and pepper on both sides, then dredge both sides in the flour. Tap off any excess.

2. Heat a large skillet over high heat and add enough oil to lightly coat the entire surface of the pan. When the oil starts to shimmer and even lets off a wisp of smoke, add the trout fillets, skin-side down, and cook until the skin is crispy and golden and the flesh has nearly all turned opaque, anywhere from 2 to 5 minutes depending on the thickness of the fillets. In case it helps: The fish is cooking almost entirely on this first side. To finish, flip and sear the other side until just cooked through, 30 seconds to 1 minute. Plate the fish and set aside.

3. In the empty pan (don't clean it out), splash in the white wine and lemon juice and cook down over medium-high heat until reduced significantly and pretty syrupy, about 3 minutes. Turn off the heat and add the butter, swirling the pan or using a wooden spoon to keep the butter moving until it's completely incorporated into the white wine and lemon juice and becomes a lovely, glossy emulsion. Pour this lemon butter over the fillets.

4. To serve, strew some capers and dill over the plates of trout and serve with white rice, which tastes divine when its edges are soaked in the lemon butter.

Maeuntang

Our family's version of maeuntang, a hot, brothy fish stew full of spices and vegetables, might look more bare bones than other recipes out there. That's because it's the kind of dish we made on fishing trips, when access to our full daily pantry was minimal. After a long day on the water, we'd catch some lake trout or, if we were at the ocean, flounder, and turn the fish into this comforting stew to feed the crowd of cousins, aunts, and uncles. Many cultures have a fish stew like this; this one is especially brothy and fresh-tasting, the flavor relying heavily on the fish itself—bone-in, skin-on fish, with the head—and just a small handful of supporting characters: radish for sweetness, gochugaru for heat, soy sauce and fish sauce for seasoning, and a bitter green to balance everything out. A smaller-scale whole fish like trout is perfect for this, since you get the benefit of the bones (and the head) without having to make a huge vat of the stuff.

6 ounces Korean radish, thinly sliced into roughly 1-inch squares

2 tablespoons gochugaru

2 tablespoons soup soy sauce (see page 23)

1 teaspoon toasted sesame oil

2 large garlic cloves, finely grated

½-inch piece fresh ginger, finely grated

1 whole trout (about 10 ounces), scaled, gutted, and cut crosswise into 3 or 4 portions

1 tablespoon fish sauce, plus more to taste

1 small yellow onion, halved and thickly sliced

Kosher salt

Large handful of mixed bitter greens, such as perilla, watercress, minari), and ssukgat (chrysanthemum greens)

Cooked white rice (page 128), for serving

SERVES 2

1. In a large pot, combine the radish, gochugaru, soup soy sauce, and sesame oil. Set over medium heat and sauté the radish, stirring occasionally, until fragrant and the gochugaru has dyed the radish red, 1 to 2 minutes. (Be careful not to burn the gochugaru.)

2. Add the garlic, ginger, trout, fish sauce, and 2 cups water and bring to a boil over high heat. Add the onion slices and continue boiling the stew until the fish is cooked through and opaque and the onions are softened, about 10 minutes. Remove from the heat.

3. Season to taste with salt and more fish sauce, if you'd like. Stir in the greens, letting them wilt, and serve immediately with white rice.

Old Bay Shrimp Cocktail
with Wasabi Chojang

Growing up, we had many a crab boil at Wrightsville Beach in North Carolina. Those dinners were Old Bay–dusted, and the smell of the spices—the celery salt, pepper, and paprika—always takes me back to those beach trips with family. I took these familiar flavors to season shrimp cocktail, one of my favorite dishes. The dipping sauce, chojang, is reminiscent of cocktail sauce, but with wasabi as the horseradish element. My brother Kevin came up with the idea at Christmas dinner one year when I assigned him the appetizer component of our menu. My dear friend (and one of this book's recipe testers) Rebecca Firkser likes serving this with lots of lemons and over ice, a nice touch because it keeps the shrimp's temperature extra cold. And if you've ever had a chilled, perfectly cooked shrimp (note: absolutely tender and almost undercooked), then you should try this.

FOR THE SHRIMP COCKTAIL

Ice cubes, as needed

¼ cup Old Bay Seasoning

2 large lemons

1 pound tail-on jumbo shrimp (16 to 20 shrimp), peeled and deveined

FOR THE WASABI CHOJANG

2 tablespoons ketchup

1 tablespoon gochujang

Juice of 1 lemon

1 teaspoon wasabi paste

SERVES 6 TO 8

1. Prepare an ice bath in a medium bowl.

2. Make the shrimp cocktail: In a large pot, combine 8 cups cold water and the Old Bay. Halve one of the lemons, squeeze both halves into the pot, and chuck them in. Bring the pot to a boil over high heat.

3. Turn the heat off and add the shrimp, stirring occasionally until they're no longer gray and have *just* begun to pink up, anywhere from 30 seconds to 2 minutes. Watch the shrimp carefully (they cook quicker than you think).

4. Once the shrimp begin to turn pink, immediately transfer them to the ice bath to halt the cooking. Once they're chilled, drain them and set them aside while you prepare the wasabi chojang.

5. Make the wasabi chojang: In a small bowl, whisk together the ketchup, gochujang, lemon juice, and wasabi.

6. To serve, fill a large platter with ice cubes and place the chilled shrimp over the ice. Cut the remaining lemon into quarters and cut each quarter in half crosswise so you're left with 8 squat wedges. Serve the lemons alongside the shrimp and wasabi chojang.

Roasted Lobster Tails
with Lemony Green Salad

In high school, on weekend shopping trips to Buckhead, my mother and I often lunched at this one restaurant called Twist. It always felt special, not just because it was a nice-ish restaurant with white tablecloths and good food, but because it was just the two of us. Our lunch dates usually consisted of tuna tataki pizzas and a salad we both adored and ordered every time: lobster with Bibb lettuce.

I tried to re-create that meal here, but in the form of lobster tails (a treat to be sure). I find it incredibly satisfying to pull out the raw lobster meat and bulk it up with delicious things like scallions, lemon zest, and soy sauce; this savory filling gets stuffed back into the shells and roasted. (Anything that gets seasoned and stuffed back into itself is fun food, in my book, and should be protected at all costs.) Roasting the tails in the oven means you end up with charred edges and plump, tender, *just*-cooked lobster. Oh, and the flying fish roe and mayonnaise combo may sound random, but it's a classic preparation for baked mussels in Korean cooking—and happens to work especially well with sweet lobster meat.

FOR THE LOBSTER

4 lobster tails

¼ cup mayonnaise

¼ cup orange flying fish roe

1 teaspoon soy sauce

2 teaspoons toasted sesame oil

2 large scallions, thinly sliced

Grated zest of 2 lemons

FOR THE SALAD

2 tablespoons fresh lemon juice

1 teaspoon Dijon mustard

2 teaspoons honey

1 tablespoon toasted sesame oil

Kosher salt and freshly ground black pepper

2 heads Bibb lettuce, leaves separated and torn into bite-size pieces

½ small red onion, thinly sliced

SERVES 2 TO 4

1. Preheat the oven to 450°F.

2. Prepare the lobster: Turn the lobster tails over. Using kitchen shears, cut alongside both edges of the tail, beginning at the side that was once connected to the body and snipping down to the tip of the tail to remove the softer undershell of the lobster tail. The lobster meat should easily slip out. Roughly chop it and add it to a medium bowl.

3. Add the mayonnaise, fish roe, soy sauce, sesame oil, scallions, and lemon zest to the lobster and toss to coat. Evenly divide the filling among the four empty tails and place the tails on a sheet pan. Roast the lobster until just cooked through and slightly caramelized on top and at the edges, 15 to 20 minutes.

4. Meanwhile, make the salad: In a small bowl, whisk together the lemon juice, mustard, honey, and sesame oil. Season to taste with salt and pepper. Place the Bibb lettuce and red onion in a large salad bowl. Drizzle the vinaigrette over the lettuce and toss with clean hands.

5. Serve the salad alongside the lobster tails.

Ganjang Gejang

Ganjang gejang, or raw crab marinated in soy sauce, is a delicacy in Korean cuisine—and is easily one of the most sought-after dishes for many Koreans, not least because it can be hard to find on a restaurant menu and is certainly not the *easiest* thing to make on the regular. To make this dish requires three things: 1) fresh blue crabs, which we often had access to thanks to our fishing trips to North Carolina; 2) the confidence to kill the critters yourself (not unlike killing a lobster), because you really need them fresh when you're eating them raw; and 3) an open mind.

Luckily the rewards are plenty. What happens as you marinate raw blue crabs is alchemy: The flesh cures in the soy sauce and becomes stained and luscious both in flavor and in texture, a softer set than ceviche. Even better if you can get female crabs with that Fanta-orange roe, which tastes like salty butter, especially when stirred into fresh white rice. In fact, Koreans call this dish "rice thief" because it's so salty and delicious that it makes you chase each bite with rice over and over to balance the wonder in your mouth. The rice provides relief from all that intensity and helps you go in for more crab. Rinse, lather, repeat.

4 large jalapeños—3 halved lengthwise, 1 thinly sliced for garnish

4 large garlic cloves, peeled

2-inch piece fresh ginger, thickly sliced

1 large yellow onion, halved and thickly sliced

1 red apple, halved and thickly sliced

1 (5-inch) square dasima (dried kelp; see page 23)

2 cups soy sauce

2 tablespoons maesil cheong (green plum syrup; see page 22)

2 tablespoons dark brown sugar

2 pounds live blue crabs (see Note)

Cooked white rice (page 128), for serving

SERVES 4

1. In a large pot, combine the 3 halved jalapeños, garlic, ginger, onion, apple, dasima, soy sauce, maesil cheong, brown sugar, and 4 cups cold water. Bring to a boil over high heat. Reduce the heat to medium-low and simmer until the brine is imbued with the aromatics, about 15 minutes. Set aside to allow the mixture to cool completely.

2. Meanwhile, place the live crabs in the freezer for 15 minutes to numb them slightly. Remove from the freezer and work quickly and confidently to euthanize the crabs. Turn each crab over on its back and, with a sharp chef's knife, pierce the center of the abdomen where the heart is, slicing downward without cutting through to the top shell.

3. With confidence, pull the top shell off and set it aside. Using kitchen shears, remove the eyes, antennae, and gills (the long, spongy organs) from the bottom section. Scrub the shells with a brush or paper towel. Repeat until all of the crabs have been cleaned.

4. Place the cleaned crab parts, both shells and bottom sections, in a 1-gallon jar or plastic tub (with a lid). Strain the cooled soy brine into the jar or tub. Cover tightly and refrigerate, allowing the crabs to marinate for at least 24 hours and up to 2 days. (If you don't plan to eat all the crabs this quickly and want them to last longer, see the Tip below.)

5. To serve, remove the crab pieces from the marinade and, if desired, use kitchen shears to cut the bottom sections in half for easier eating. Garnish with the remaining thinly sliced jalapeño and serve with white rice, which can be rubbed into the shells to mop up all of the roe and flesh inside.

Note You can buy live blue crabs from a fishmonger, in the summer especially, or do what I do: Call your local Korean supermarket in advance and ask when they're getting their shipment of live crabs. I ask them to hold a couple pounds for me (and to please not kill them yet), and they always oblige. Or you could always go crabbing, which is super fun.

Tip If you want to hold the crabs for more than 2 days (and up to a week), then on the second or third day, strain the soy sauce brine from the jar into a pot (leaving the crabs in their container in the fridge). Bring the brine to a strong boil for 5 minutes, skimming off any impurities that rise to the surface. Cool the brine completely before pouring it back over the crabs. For extra safety, if Jean keeps the crabs for longer than three days, she does this one more time on day four or five.

Garden of Jean
The vegetable chapter

Every house we've ever bought has had a garden bigger than the previous one. I'm waiting for my parents to buy a farm next—not to run a business, but to accommodate Jean's ever-expanding garden. In the backyard of her home in the suburbs of Atlanta, my mother has a plot where she grows everything from blueberries and bell peppers to perilla, mint, scallions, garlic chives, various lettuces, and jalapeños, too, of course. And if you notice a deluge of cucumber and tomato recipes here, that's because Jean grows and eats bushels of them throughout the summer. They grow like wildfire in Georgia. On my most recent drive up to New York from Atlanta, for the entire ride I snacked on cucumbers and cherry tomatoes that she packed for me in little ziplock bags. I've become so used to her summer bounty that I probably take it for granted that our house is always brimming with both.

I wanted to feature my mother's garden in this chapter on vegetables not just because she grows so many cool things, but also because I feel that it's a great metaphor for Korean home cooking: When people think of Korean food, they often think of grilled meats and big fleshy stews. But it's more vegetable-heavy than people realize, especially at home. And if *I'm* telling you to make a vegetable dish, then it must be pretty good. As a carnivore, I never thought I'd be developing so many recipes starring vegetables, but these were some of the most exciting to write because they show off the versatility of my mother's kitchen, her garden, and how a pantry stocked with Korean essentials (page 21) can power up even the simplest of nature's treasures.

Oi Naengguk
with Heirloom Cherry Tomatoes

When my mom makes this chilled soup in the summer to use up her massive cucumber and tomato stash, we have it almost like a cool drink with a meal of rice and other dishes. It's that refreshing. Of course, once you get to the bottom of the naengguk (cold soup), the remaining crunchy vegetables, including the oi (cucumber), are so infused with sharp, salty-sweet flavors that they're like little pickles themselves: a bright, hydrating finish.

1 large garlic clove, finely grated

1 teaspoon kosher salt

2 tablespoons sugar

¼ cup distilled white vinegar

1 tablespoon maesil cheong (green plum syrup; see page 22), plus more to taste

1 tablespoon soup soy sauce (see page 23), plus more to taste

½ pound Persian (mini) cucumbers, cut into matchsticks

10 heirloom cherry tomatoes, halved

1 large scallion, thinly sliced on the diagonal

1 tablespoon toasted sesame seeds

2 cups crushed ice

SERVES 4

1. In a medium bowl, combine 2 cups cold tap water, the garlic, salt, sugar, vinegar, plum syrup, and soup soy sauce. Stir until the salt and sugar are dissolved. Add the cucumbers, tomatoes, scallion, and sesame seeds. Taste for seasoning, adding more maesil cheong for sweetness and soup soy sauce for saltiness, keeping in mind that the ice will dilute this later. It should taste strong but drinkable.

2. Just before serving, add the crushed ice, then ladle into small bowls, making sure to get a little vegetable, soup, and ice in each portion.

Chicken Radishes

Every time I make these, my brother whispers, "Chocolate Boy." If you grew up in the '90s, like we did, then you may have watched the critically acclaimed Nickelodeon show *Hey Arnold!* In one episode (that I'm now realizing had really dark undertones), a strung-out kid who goes by "Chocolate Boy" is able to curb his cocoa addiction by replacing it with raw red radishes. Of course, what's implied is that he's now addicted to the radishes.

These chicken radishes *are* especially easy to eat and taste great with the dish they're meant to be eaten with: Korean fried chicken (page 239). It makes sense. When you're eating something rich like fried food, you want a sharp, refreshing pickle to go with. In the Korean way, this one has more sugar than you think you'll need, not least to offset the wonderful bitterness of the radishes. Borrowing from chicken mu, a quick pickle made from cubed white Korean radish, my version uses toy-bright red radishes, one of my favorite things to eat, and something I can't seem to wean from my diet even if I tried.

10 to 12 ounces red radishes, trimmed and cleaned, any large radishes halved

½ cup distilled white vinegar

½ cup sugar

1 tablespoon kosher salt

MAKES 1 PINT

1. Place the radishes in a pint jar or other resealable pickling container.

2. In a large spouted measuring cup, whisk together 1 cup cold water, the vinegar, sugar, and salt until dissolved. Pour this solution into the jar with the radishes. It should cover the radishes. Seal the jar and refrigerate the radishes overnight before serving. This keeps for up to 1 week in the refrigerator, after which they'll start to wrinkle and get sad.

One Dressing, a Thousand Fruit Muchims

The first thing I'll say is this: A lot of things we think are vegetables in this world are actually fruits (tomatoes, cucumbers, zucchini, and peppers, for instance). Now that we got that out of the way, there's a reason why I love this all-purpose dressing on fresh fruits of all varieties: When the fruit is good and sweet, adding salt, heat, and nuttiness rounds it out and turns it into an incredible side salad. These muchims, or dressed salads, would taste great on any menu, but my favorite way to eat them is straight from a big bowl on a porch in the summer.

FOR THE FRUIT

1 pound fruit, cut into bite-size pieces (like tomatoes, cucumbers, zucchini, sweet peppers, watermelon, cantaloupe, honeydew, pineapple, mangoes, peaches, plums, pears, apples, or cherries, stemmed, seeded, and/or cored)

1 teaspoon kosher salt

FOR THE DRESSING

2 tablespoons distilled white vinegar

1 large garlic clove, finely grated

1 tablespoon plus 1 teaspoon toasted sesame oil

1 tablespoon gochugaru

2 teaspoons fish sauce

1 teaspoon sugar

MAKES 2½ CUPS

1. **Prepare the fruit:** In a medium bowl, toss the fruit with the salt, transfer the fruit to a colander, and let sit in the sink to drain, about 30 minutes.

2. **Meanwhile, make the dressing:** In the same bowl you just used for the fruit, combine the vinegar and garlic and set aside for 30 minutes to allow the garlic to mellow.

3. After 30 minutes, to the vinegar and garlic mixture, add the sesame oil, gochugaru, fish sauce, and sugar and whisk to combine.

4. Use a paper or cloth kitchen towel to pat the fruit dry, then add to the dressing and toss until well coated. This muchim is best eaten right away, but can be refrigerated for up to 48 hours, after which the bright flavors will start to mute and the dressing will break down the fruit.

RECIPE CONTINUES

Variation: Raw Brussels Sprout Muchim

I don't know that I'll ever roast another Brussels sprout again. Turns out raw sprouts taste wonderful as a muchim, too, their crunchy bitterness offset by the spicy-sweet gochugaru dressing.

To make it, follow the recipe for One Dressing, a Thousand Fruit Muchims (page 187). In step 1, replace the fruit with ½ pound Brussels sprouts, trimmed and thinly sliced, and reduce the salt to ½ teaspoon. Follow the rest of the recipe as directed.

Garlicky Creamed Spinach Namul

Let's get one thing straight: People are *passionate* about sigeumchi namul, a simple banchan of spinach sautéed with garlic, salt, and sesame oil, sometimes soy sauce. When I polled my readers for their favorite banchan, that was by far the most requested recipe. There are plenty of great versions out there, so I wanted to offer something that I enjoy eating, which is: iron-rich spinach that's been drowned in cream and seasoned with all those same delicious namul flavorings. Though I won't claim that this is sigeumchi namul, the result is something comforting and familiar, somewhere between the creamed spinach you might order alongside a steak and the banchan you reach for whenever you're craving greens and Mom's cooking.

1 pound frozen chopped spinach, thawed

½ cup heavy cream

4 large garlic cloves, finely grated

2 tablespoons soy sauce

2 teaspoons toasted sesame oil

2 teaspoons sugar

¼ cup toasted sesame seeds, plus more for serving

SERVES 4

1. Preheat the oven to 425°F.

2. Squeeze the spinach with your hands over the sink to wring out as much water as possible.

3. Add the spinach to a small braiser or baking dish along with the cream, garlic, soy sauce, sesame oil, sugar, and sesame seeds. Stir to combine.

4. Bake the spinach, uncovered, until the spinach is warmed through, about 15 minutes. Serve warm garnished with more sesame seeds.

Gem Lettuce Salad
with Roasted-Seaweed Vinaigrette

Little Gems are adorable—sturdier, sweeter, and more flavorful versions of their cousin, crunchy romaine (which are also good and have their place in the pantheon of lettuces). I love how meaty Little Gems are, and how one head of their leaves equates to the perfect side salad for one, or maybe two smaller servings. Which means: This recipe is very easy to scale up.

And rather than whisk the vinaigrette together first, I like to splash the leaves with each dressing ingredient individually, mostly out of laziness, but also because that way you can visualize how much you're seasoning the leaves. We season everything else like this—why not lettuce? Also, there's powdered gim (seasoned roasted seaweed) in here because, well, it's me.

1 (5-gram) packet gim

1 head Little Gem lettuce (5 to 6 ounces), leaves separated

1 tablespoon rice vinegar

1 tablespoon fish sauce

1 tablespoon toasted sesame oil

Pinch of sugar

Kosher salt and freshly ground black pepper

MAKES 1 LARGE SALAD

1. In a spice grinder or food processor, grind the gim into a powder.

2. On a large plate, scatter the Little Gem lettuce leaves in a single layer and splash them with the rice vinegar, fish sauce, sesame oil, and sugar. Season lightly with salt and heavily with black pepper. Sprinkle the gim powder all over the leaves. Serve immediately.

Smashed Potatoes
with Roasted-Seaweed Sour Cream Dip

If there's one word to describe the transcendent combo of sour cream and gim, it would be: gosohae, or nutty (like from toasted sesame oil). There's something, too, about fat—and cream, in particular—that helps the savoriness of roasted seaweed come through. Blended into sour cream with garlic, rice vinegar, and a healthy dribble of toasted sesame oil, roasted seaweed makes for one of the most satisfying, umami-rich dips. This is my go-to party appetizer. You can choose your own adventure here: Serve this dip smeared beneath a plate of crispy roasted smashed potatoes or alongside a platter of rainbow crudités (see Variation on page 194).

FOR THE SMASHED POTATOES

1½ pounds fingerling potatoes

¼ cup olive oil, plus more as needed

¼ teaspoon garlic powder

Kosher salt and freshly ground black pepper

FOR THE SOUR CREAM DIP

8 ounces sour cream (about 1 cup)

2 (5-gram) packets gim

1 large garlic clove, finely grated

1 tablespoon rice vinegar

2 teaspoons toasted sesame oil, plus more to taste

1 teaspoon kosher salt, plus more to taste

½ teaspoon freshly ground black pepper, plus more to taste

1 teaspoon sugar

2 large scallions, thinly sliced on the diagonal

SERVES 4

1. Preheat the oven to 425°F.

2. Make the potatoes: Lay the potatoes on a sheet pan in a single layer and roast dry (without oil or salt!) until soft enough to smash, about 30 minutes.

3. Remove the pan from the oven and, using the flat bottom of a drinking glass, press on each potato to smash them slightly. Drizzle the potatoes with the olive oil, sprinkle with the garlic powder, and season with salt and pepper. Use a spatula to toss everything together so the smashed potato pieces are well seasoned.

4. Return to the oven and bake until crispy, about 30 minutes longer.

5. Meanwhile, as the potatoes roast, make the sour cream dip: In a food processor, blitz the sour cream, gim, garlic, vinegar, sesame oil, salt, pepper, and sugar until smooth. Taste and adjust seasonings as desired.

6. To serve, slather a large platter with the sour cream dip and arrange the crispy smashed potatoes over it. Messily scatter the scallions over the top and serve immediately.

RECIPE CONTINUES

Variation: Crudités with Roasted-Seaweed Sour Cream Dip

You could also leave the oven off and serve this dip as part of a crudités platter instead.

To make it, follow the recipe for Smashed Potatoes with Roasted-Seaweed Sour Cream Dip (page 193), but skip the potatoes and just make the sour cream dip in step 5. Transfer the sour cream dip to a small bowl and place on a large platter. Arrange an assortment of raw, crunchy, and preferably bitter vegetables (like radishes, endive, and radicchio), cleaned and trimmed, on the platter, sprinkling them with a fat pinch of kosher or flaky sea salt.

Grilled Trumpet Mushrooms
with Ssamjang

When I'm grilling outside or having a Korean barbecue night at home, I always make sure to buy some king trumpet mushrooms. I love their meatiness when grilled, even more when they've been brushed with ssamjang, a funky, flavorful condiment that tastes great in lettuce wraps. I'm not saying that vegetables *have* to taste like meat to be good. By "meatiness," what I really mean is umami, which ssamjang is loaded with. Especially when brushed onto a warm, just-cooked mushroom, it sort of glistens up and makes the vegetable shine in all the right ways.

FOR THE SSAMJANG

1 teaspoon doenjang (see page 23)

½ teaspoon gochujang

1 large garlic clove, finely grated

1 teaspoon vinegar

1 teaspoon honey

4 large trumpet mushrooms, cut lengthwise into ¼-inch-thick slices

Vegetable oil

Kosher salt and freshly ground black pepper

SERVES 4

1. Prepare an outdoor grill for direct high-heat cooking, or heat a large grill pan over high.

2. In a small bowl or dish, stir together the doenjang, gochujang, garlic, 1 teaspoon water, the vinegar, and honey. Set the ssamjang aside.

3. Massage the mushrooms with enough oil to coat, then season with salt and pepper. Grill until golden brown and slightly charred at the edges, about 2 minutes on the first side. Turn the mushrooms over and grill on the second side until golden brown and slightly charred as well, about 1 minute more. Transfer to a platter.

4. Use a silicone basting brush (or a spoon) to coat the mushrooms with the ssamjang. Or you can serve the ssamjang on the side of the mushrooms as a dipping sauce, which is also nice.

PHOTO NEXT PAGE

Crispy Yangnyeom Chickpeas
with Caramelized Honey

Sticky-sweet yangnyeom sauce is one of those genius inventions that was meant for fried chicken, but tastes wonderful on everything else—case in point, crispy chickpeas. To be truly happy, this is all I need with Netflix, a cold beer, and my pup at my side. And like most things in this book, these chickpeas taste divine as a banchan with a little fresh white rice on the side. The scallions are also a nod to a particular preparation of fried chicken in Korea, where a tangle of them is added atop for freshness. Don't skip the caramelized honey: It's really fun to make and finishes the dish with a shiny gloss, plus the sweetness helps balance the other flavors, like the funky heat from the gochujang and the savory bite from the soy sauce and garlic.

1 (15-ounce) can chickpeas, drained, rinsed, and dried on a paper towel

2 tablespoons olive oil

Kosher salt and freshly ground black pepper

3 tablespoons ketchup

1 tablespoon gochujang

1 tablespoon strawberry jam

1 tablespoon soy sauce

1 tablespoon minced garlic

1 tablespoon honey

1 tablespoon toasted sesame seeds

2 large scallions, julienned into long thin strips, soaked in iced water (see Tip)

SERVES 4

1. Preheat the oven to 400°F.

2. On a sheet pan, toss the chickpeas with the olive oil and a few pinches of salt and pepper. Bake until crispy, 25 to 30 minutes, shaking the pan halfway through baking.

3. Meanwhile, in a small saucepan or skillet, combine the ketchup, gochujang, strawberry jam, soy sauce, and garlic and bring to a gentle simmer over medium-high heat, stirring constantly. Cook this yangnyeom sauce until fragrant, about 1 minute.

4. Add the crispy chickpeas to the pan and continue to cook, stirring constantly, until the sauce reduces slightly and gets absorbed by the chickpeas, and the chickpeas get sticky, 2 to 3 minutes.

5. Move the chickpeas to one side of the pan and add the honey to the empty side. Let the honey bubble up, stirring all the while, and cook down until reduced and caramelized, about 1 minute or so. Stir the chickpeas into the honey and watch as they glisten up. Remove from the heat.

6. To serve, transfer the chickpeas to a plate and sprinkle with the sesame seeds and scallions.

Tip Soaking long strands of scallions in ice-cold water will cause them to curl like the photo on page 198. This garnish doesn't make or break the dish by any means, but it does looks fun and adds volume and freshness to the plate. The icy soak softens the oniony bite from the scallions, allowing you to eat them like a salad.

Charred Cauliflower
with Magic Gochugaru Dust

Here's a simple preparation that lets cauliflower shine. And you really want to char the vegetable if you can, since that flavor tastes so wonderful with the smoky paprika and fruity gochugaru in my all-purpose spice blend, which I've coined "magic" because it turns anything you dust it over into an instant lip-smacking side dish (looks cool, too). Try this magic dust over roasted broccoli, cabbage, Brussels sprouts, what have you.

2 teaspoons kosher salt

1 teaspoon gochugaru

½ teaspoon smoked paprika

¼ teaspoon dark brown sugar

¼ teaspoon garlic powder

1 head cauliflower (about 2 pounds), preferably with leaves, sliced into large florets

Vegetable oil

SERVES 4

1. In a small bowl, stir together the salt, gochugaru, smoked paprika, brown sugar, and garlic powder. Set the gochugaru dust aside.

2. Position an oven rack in the highest position and preheat the broiler.

3. Arrange the cauliflower on a sheet pan in a single layer, drizzle with oil, and gently toss. Broil until the edges are charred, anywhere from 5 to 15 minutes, depending on your broiler. (Watch it carefully so it doesn't burn.)

4. Arrange the charred cauliflower florets on a large plate and dust generously with the gochugaru dust.

Gochujang-Glazed Zucchini
with Fried Scallions

This preparation of vegetables (or, rather, fruits, since zucchini are technically fruits) is near and dear to my heart because it was the first time in my career that I saw a recipe of mine go viral. People cooked this; and even more, they started riffing on the base vegetable, which made me so happy. Originally published in *The New York Times* using eggplant, this recipe stars zucchini that tastes best just barely cooked, perhaps with a little char, but mostly still raw and crunchy inside. The fried scallions are worth the extra effort—trust me.

1 pound zucchini, ends trimmed, halved lengthwise, and cut on the diagonal into 4- to 5-inch segments

1 teaspoon kosher salt

2 tablespoons gochujang

1 tablespoon soy sauce

2 teaspoons dark brown sugar

1 teaspoon toasted sesame oil

2 large garlic cloves, finely grated

4 large scallions

½ cup vegetable oil

SERVES 4

1. Place the zucchini in a colander set inside a large bowl or the sink. Sprinkle with the salt, toss, and let sit for 30 minutes to drain slightly.

2. Meanwhile, in a small bowl, whisk together the gochujang, soy sauce, brown sugar, sesame oil, and garlic. Set the gochujang sauce aside.

3. Cut the scallions crosswise into 3-inch segments, then slice each segment lengthwise into thin strips. Keep the white and green parts separate.

4. In a large skillet, combine the vegetable oil and scallion whites. Set the pan over medium heat and fry the scallions, stirring often, until beginning to brown, 4 to 5 minutes. Add the scallion greens to the hot oil and cook until all of the scallions are crispy and lightly browned, 3 to 4 minutes longer. Transfer the fried scallions to a paper towel.

5. Remove the skillet from the heat and carefully pour the hot scallion oil into a glass container or measuring cup.

6. After the 30 minutes of salting, dry the zucchini with a cloth or paper towel. Return the skillet to medium-high heat and add 2 tablespoons of the reserved scallion oil. When the oil starts to shimmer and you see a wisp of smoke, add the zucchini, cut-sides down, and fry until slightly charred but still bright green and crunchy, 2 to 3 minutes. Flip once and cook on the other side until slightly charred at the edges, about 1 more minute.

7. Remove from the heat and pour the reserved gochujang sauce over the zucchini. Toss until evenly coated and the gochujang starts to thicken and get glossy in the residual heat of the pan, about 1 minute.

8. Plate the zucchini on a large platter and garnish with the fried scallions. Serve immediately.

Feasts
Menus and ruminations
on living

What is a feast if not a meal persevering? When I think of feasts, I think of long, leisurely dinners, ones filled with family and friends gathered around a couple big tables. Feasts should be full of joy (the word "feast" actually comes from the Latin *festus*, meaning "joyous"). If the TV dinners, stews, and rice dishes earlier in this book showcase my family's daily home cooking, then these feasts are about our occasions: the messy, disorganized hodgepodge Thanksgiving (page 208), with influences that span time and space; the Argentine empanada-folding party (page 222) that my mom and I have, just the two of us, every Christmas; and the Korean fried chicken (page 239) we always chase with soju and beer because that's just the way we do it.

And it's not that these meals themselves require more time to cook, but that we create more time to eat them. When we create rituals out of pleasure, like we do with holiday foods, we look forward to them that much more. And what could be more comforting than repetition? Even better when a food tradition is specific to a family, because that means it has a singular story that no one else shares. There's a reason japchae (page 231) and kalbi (page 232) make me think of parties as much as a big roast chicken (page 210): The return on these dishes is as high as the investment (both physical and emotional), which makes their recipes especially precious. Jean's kalbi tastes best when it's been marinated for days (don't let anyone tell you otherwise). The empanadas take patience (and practice) to fold prettily. The scallion stuffing (page 212) requires day-old bread that you start drying out the night before. Time is a main ingredient in so much of my family's cooking, but especially in our festal food.

When it comes to family, time has always been of the essence. Feasts aren't just about celebrating for the sake of celebrating; they are opportunities to stop and acknowledge the simple act of being alive. In my family, celebrating a birthday is the same as celebrating the day of someone's passing, as many Koreans do in the form of jesa, an ancestral rite. When mourning a lost loved one, people say to think of it as celebrating the life of that person rather than lamenting their death, but I'd go one step further: Celebrate that you loved someone so much that their loss has created a hole in you. As humans, we like to brush off our scars, but sometimes they're the only evidence we have left of the people who matter most to us, and the people who will eventually leave us. Even at jesa, there's food. Nigella Lawson says it best in my favorite book of hers, *Feast*: "I am not someone who believes that life is sacred, but I know it is very precious. To turn away from that, to act as if living

is immaterial, that what you need to sustain life doesn't count, is to repudiate and diminish the tragedy of the loss of a life."

Eating, then, can be one way to honor the dead. And therein lies the magic of feasting: spending time on an act that we, the living, often take for granted. Food couldn't be more of a repudiation of death. It's an act of the living— and it's we the living who understand most how precious, and short, life can be.

A Korean American Thanksgiving

Thanksgiving for me feels almost like another family member. She's that long-lost cousin you only see once a year, but when you do, you're so happy to catch up. It was the first holiday that really felt like something we as a family could call our own—because it was our table, and we could cook whatever we wanted. That's the fun thing about Thanksgiving: There's a general framework (a bird, a potato, a stuffing, a casserole, at least one green vegetable . . .), but otherwise the meal looks the way it does today because family members kept requesting repeats of their favorites, and now those favorites are annual classics.

Thanksgiving didn't mean much to us as kids—it wasn't until we were old enough to cook the meal ourselves that it resonated. I remember at thirteen years old, for instance, cooking full Thanksgiving meals with my older cousins while the parents sat in the living room getting drunk, gossiping, and playing cards. In a way, it became a nice tradition, a generational role reversal: Thanksgiving was the one day of the year that the parents got to sit back and relax while the kids took care of dinner, not least because none of the adults knew how to make American food.

One aspect about growing up as a child of immigrants is that I know how to cook the American stuff that my mother doesn't, and she knows how to cook the Korean stuff that I don't. Ideally there should be an exchange of that knowledge between generations, which was the main goal while writing this book. But that's the trap when it comes to ritualistic meals like Thanksgiving: Sometimes the reason that something becomes tradition—and even more, a family recipe—is because of the emotional attachment you have to the first person who made the dish and gave you those feelings of joy. So as long as the person is still alive, that dish will always exist from their hands. But what happens when they pass?

There are many reasons to write down recipes, not just so you can eat the food again, but also so you can keep the memory of loved ones with you forever. Still, that's the purpose of writing down a recipe, right? As humans, we hold on to the hope that through food, and through the passing down of recipes through generations, we can preserve a life.

I don't know if I'll be immortalized thanks to my Thanksgiving menu, but I do feel that Thanksgiving is, for my family, the ultimate Korean American feast. After having cooked nearly twenty-two Thanksgivings now, the one piece of advice I have is this: Make most of the casseroles the night before so that Thanksgiving Day can be dedicated to the bird and the fun appetizers, maybe even a pie or two if you have time. But if you don't have time to make a pie, or a galette as I share here, store-bought is fine—as is, I don't know, a plate of cut persimmons.

The Kim Family Thanksgiving Menu

Yangnyeom Roast Chicken (page 210)

Cheesy Scallion Stuffing with Sesame Seeds (page 212)

Sesame-Soy Deviled Eggs (page 215)

Aunt Anne's Broccoli-Cheese Rice Casserole (page 216)

Mac-and-Corn-Cheese with Jalapeño Bread Crumbs (page 219)

Honey-Buttered Goguma Casserole with Turmeric (page 220)

Raw Brussels Sprout Muchim (page 188)

Gem Lettuce Salad with Roasted-Seaweed Vinaigrette (page 190)

**Korean Pear Galette with Salted Cinnamon
Whipped Cream** (page 259)

All of the cousins together on Thanksgiving Day,
sometime in the early 1990s.

Yangnyeom Roast Chicken

Though you could swap a turkey for this roast chicken, in those earlier Thanksgivings when all the teenagers in my family cooked the big feast on our own, we often just roasted a chicken—sometimes two, if the guest list was long. Turkey was expensive and always made us go over budget, and back then we didn't really know how to roast one anyway, so we stuck to what we knew and what we liked (which was chicken). I won't pretend that our Thanksgiving roast chickens tasted anything like this; they were usually simpler salt-and-pepper birds. But as an adult, I now find that brushing the sticky, spicy-sweet yangnyeom sauce normally found on Korean fried chicken, makes for an incredible centerpiece bird that glistens red.

1 whole chicken (3 to 4 pounds)

Olive oil

Kosher salt and freshly ground black pepper

¼ cup ketchup

2 tablespoons maple syrup

1 tablespoon gochujang

1 tablespoon strawberry jam

1 tablespoon dark brown sugar

3 large garlic cloves, finely grated

SERVES 4 TO 6

1. Preheat the oven to 425°F.

2. Place the chicken on a sheet pan (the best vessel for crisping up a roast chicken) breast-side up and rub it with olive oil. Season all sides, crevasses, and inside the cavity with salt and pepper.

3. Roast the chicken for 45 minutes to 1 hour, or until the juices at the thigh joint run clear and the meat reaches 165°F. (Another trick is to just multiply the weight of your chicken by 15; in other words, go for about 15 minutes per pound.)

4. Meanwhile, in a medium bowl, whisk together the ketchup, maple syrup, gochujang, strawberry jam, brown sugar, and garlic. Set the yangnyeom sauce aside.

5. Once the chicken is done roasting, remove the pan from the oven and transfer the bird to a wooden cutting board and rest for at least 10 minutes.

6. Brush the chicken with the yangnyeom sauce and carve.

Cheesy Scallion Stuffing
with Sesame Seeds

This stuffing is full of umami, thanks to seven scallions, which are gently bloomed in an entire stick of butter (hey, it's Thanksgiving), creating an aromatic base that underpins the dish. If I were to compare the flavor profile to anything, I'd say: pajeon—those wonderfully lacy, savory scallion pancakes that are often served with soy sauce for dipping. This pajeon-y stuffing is the bready thing on the table. And the act of making it is sort of a signal that Thanksgiving has officially begun.

One of my favorite parts of the whole Turkey Day experience is tearing up stale bread and letting it dry out overnight on a sheet pan so it can really soak up the eggy filling later. There's something comforting about it, knowing that so many other Americans are doing the exact same thing as you are, not just on Thanksgiving Day, but also the night before. As the cooks of their families know, night-before-Thanksgiving cooking is more leisurely and often done alone. The calm before the storm. I love that juxtaposition of quiet solo cooking against the reality of the meal: rambunctious communal feasting.

1 (12-ounce) loaf sourdough bread

1 stick (½ cup) unsalted butter, plus more for the baking dish

7 large scallions, thinly sliced on the diagonal

2 celery stalks, thinly sliced

1 large red onion, halved and thinly sliced

1 teaspoon kosher salt

1 tablespoon sugar

½ cup whole milk

2 cups turkey or vegetable stock

1 teaspoon soy sauce

1 teaspoon toasted sesame oil

2 tablespoons toasted sesame seeds, plus more for topping

1 cup coarsely grated Parmesan cheese, plus more for topping

2 large eggs

SERVES 6 TO 8

1. The night before serving, tear the bread into 1- to 2-inch pieces, removing the crusts while doing so (you should end up with about 4 cups of bread). Set the bread on a sheet pan and let dry overnight. (If making the day of, simply place the bread pieces in a 300°F oven until dried out, 30 to 50 minutes.)

2. The day of Thanksgiving, preheat the oven to 350°F and grease a 9 × 13-inch baking dish with softened butter.

3. In a large skillet, melt the 1 stick of butter over medium-high heat. Add the scallions, celery, onion, salt, and sugar. Sauté, stirring occasionally, until the vegetables begin to soften (but stay vibrant and crunchy) and the scallions have infused the butter with their wonderful flavor, about 5 minutes.

4. Transfer the vegetable mixture to a large bowl. Whisk in the milk, stock, soy sauce, sesame oil, sesame seeds, and Parmesan. Crack in the eggs and whisk to combine. Add the bread pieces and toss until evenly coated. Allow to sit for about 10 minutes to slightly soak up the egg mixture.

5. Transfer the stuffing to the greased baking dish and top with some more sesame seeds and Parmesan, as desired. (You can assemble the dish to this point ahead; see Tip.)

6. Cover with foil and bake the stuffing until cooked through, about 30 minutes, then remove the foil and continue baking until the top is slightly browned and the cheese has melted, 10 to 15 minutes.

Tip This is a great dish to prep a day or two ahead (I wouldn't do it any earlier than that, or else you'll lose control of the moisture in the bread). After assembling (and before baking), cover with foil and place in the refrigerator. You'll want to add a few minutes to the bake time, however, since it'll be colder than usual going in.

Sesame-Soy Deviled Eggs

These are the deviled eggs I make the most. They sort of taste like if you took gyerangbap, or egg rice (page 130), and turned it into a single party bite: salty from soy sauce, nutty from sesame oil, and full of deep savoriness from the roasted seaweed. My parents love these because they taste, well, Korean.

6 large eggs

¼ cup mayonnaise

1 teaspoon soy sauce

1 teaspoon toasted sesame oil, plus more as needed

Black sesame seeds, for serving

2 small sheets gim (from a 5-gram packet), for garnish

MAKES 12 EGG HALVES

1. In a small pot, place the eggs in a single layer and add cold water to cover. Bring to a boil over high heat, then immediately turn off the heat, cover, and set your timer for 15 minutes. After 15 minutes of steeping, pour the hot water out and place the pot under a cold running tap. The eggs should be cool enough to touch now. Crack the bottom of each egg on a hard surface, such as the sink or counter, and return to the cold water, letting them sit for a few seconds. Peel the eggs and halve them lengthwise.

2. Pop the yolks out into a small bowl. Add the mayonnaise, soy sauce, and sesame oil to the yolks and whisk together until smooth and fluffy. Add more sesame oil if dry. Transfer this filling to a resealable plastic bag and snip off one corner of the bag. Pipe the filling into each egg. (If making ahead, cover the eggs and keep in the fridge for up to 2 days.)

3. Right before serving, sprinkle some black sesame seeds atop each egg. Using kitchen shears, snip the gim into a dozen 1-inch squares and top each egg with a single square.

Aunt Anne's Broccoli-Cheese Rice Casserole

This is everyone's favorite casserole, not least because on Thanksgiving Day it's the only rice dish on the table (and my Korean family *loves* rice). When my cousin Becky finally learned how to make broccoli-cheese rice casserole from her Aunt Anne, whose Southern food I always thought tasted so good, she usually made two vats of it because it's the one dish everyone wants leftovers of. (It also happens to reheat especially well—a key requirement for any Thanksgiving side dish, in my book.)

What I love most is how much this recipe has changed over time. I call it *Aunt Anne's* Broccoli-Cheese Rice Casserole because she's the catalyst for the dish, but really it's "*Eric's* interpretation of *Becky's* Broccoli-Cheese Rice Casserole, which she maybe learned from her mother, *Julia*, who learned it from her sister *Anne*." Like a game of telephone, the recipe has been tweaked and misremembered, and now tastes like a mere version of that first casserole we had as kids, which is fine because we're not kids anymore. And I love that. This kind of culinary evolution is what defines Thanksgiving for me.

As for the broccoli, sometimes I like to use only florets because that's my favorite part of the vegetable, but my mother likes it the way Aunt Anne makes it, which was often with frozen chopped broccoli (stems and everything). The original had Velveeta cheese, as well, but I enjoy the sharpness of cheddar and the ease of ready-shredded cheese, which is what I call for here.

1 stick (½ cup) unsalted butter, plus more for the baking dish

1 medium red onion, diced

1 teaspoon sugar

Kosher salt and freshly ground black pepper

4 slices white sandwich bread (about 4 ounces), crusts removed and cut into bite-size pieces

2 cups cooked white rice (page 128), fresh, day-old, or cold

20 ounces frozen chopped broccoli (do not thaw)

8 ounces shredded sharp cheddar cheese (about 2 cups)

1 cup sour cream

1 cup whole milk, plus more as needed

SERVES 6 TO 8

1. Preheat the oven to 350°F. Grease a 9 × 13-inch baking dish with softened butter.

2. In a large skillet, melt the 1 stick of butter over medium-high heat. Add the onion, sprinkle with the sugar, and season with salt and pepper. Reduce the heat to medium-low and cook, stirring occasionally, until the onion is slightly caramelized, 15 to 20 minutes.

3. Add the bread to the buttery onions, increase the heat to medium, and sauté until slightly toasted, 10 to 12 minutes. Remove from the heat.

4. In your biggest bowl, use your hands to toss together the rice, frozen broccoli, cheddar, sour cream, milk, 2 teaspoons salt, and the buttery onion-bread mixture until well mixed. Spread evenly into the greased baking dish. (You can make this ahead up to this point; see Tip.)

5. Bake the casserole until bubbling, warmed through, and slightly browned at the edges, 30 to 40 minutes. Serve warm. Refrigerate leftovers in an airtight container for up to 4 days.

Tip You can prep this casserole completely in advance (just don't bake it yet) and freeze it for up to 1 month or refrigerate it for up to 3 days. Just add a few minutes to the bake time when you're ready to cook it.

Mac-and-Corn-Cheese
with Jalapeño Bread Crumbs

Macaroni and cheese is the one thing we never made from scratch. As lifelong devotees of that red Stouffer's box, we as a family still, to this day, love how creamy and dreamy that frozen mac is. But this year, I decided to develop my own Thanksgiving macaroni and cheese, something new (and homemade) our family could get excited about every year. Inspired by corn cheese, that lovely side dish that comes out sizzling at Korean restaurants, I wanted to incorporate those flavors into a dish that could feel like the mac and cheese moment on our table. This recipe tells the story of my family: By now you must know that we use jalapeño not just for heat, but also for flavor. And we love sweet corn in creamy, cheesy things. It doesn't hurt that this recipe is made entirely on the stovetop—because perhaps more than anyone, I know that oven space is at a premium on Thanksgiving.

Kosher salt

8 ounces rigatoni or other short pasta

2 tablespoons olive oil

½ cup panko bread crumbs

Freshly ground black pepper

1½ cups shredded low-moisture mozzarella cheese

½ small red onion, halved and thinly sliced

2 large jalapeños, seeded and finely diced

2 tablespoons unsalted butter

2 tablespoons all-purpose flour

1 cup whole milk

1 cup frozen corn kernels

1 tablespoon mayonnaise

Pinch of sugar

SERVES 6 TO 8

1. Bring a medium pot of water to a boil and salt it generously. Add the pasta and cook until al dente according to the package directions.

2. Meanwhile, heat a medium skillet over medium-high heat and add the olive oil. Add the panko, season with salt and pepper, and stir, toasting them until evenly browned, 2 to 3 minutes. Remove from the heat and stir in ½ cup of the mozzarella, half of the red onion, and half of the jalapeños. Let the residual heat sweat the vegetables slightly and melt the mozzarella, forming deliciously savory, granola-like cheese clusters. Set aside.

3. In a large Dutch oven, melt the butter over medium heat. Whisk in the flour, cooking it until it's smooth and pasty, about 1 minute. Whisk in the milk and increase the heat to high to bring it to a boil. Reduce the heat to medium and continue cooking, whisking constantly, until a creamy Alfredo-like sauce forms, 2 to 3 minutes. Remove from the heat, stir in the corn, mayonnaise, sugar, and the remaining 1 cup mozzarella, half of the red onion, and half of the jalapeños. Season with salt and pepper.

4. Drain the cooked pasta and add it to the sauce, stirring until combined. You can transfer the mac and cheese to a serving dish or just serve it directly from the Dutch oven. Just be sure to scatter the reserved cheesy jalapeño bread crumbs atop before serving.

Honey-Buttered Goguma Casserole
with Turmeric

Until recently when Jean started hosting holiday dinners, we only ever had sweet potato casserole at my Aunt Joy's Thanksgivings in Augusta, Georgia. I didn't know how much everyone in my family adored sweet potato casserole (yes, with marshmallows) and missed it until this most recent Thanksgiving, when I made this version with honey butter and turmeric. Now, I can't imagine another Thanksgiving without it.

People who don't understand American Thanksgiving food always laugh off the combination, but if you've ever had toasted marshmallows with a homemade sweet potato filling—even better if the sweet potato in question is goguma, the yellow-fleshed beauty that is the darling of the Korean potato world—then you know how good and comforting the sweetness can taste against the other savory flavors of the table. It's also a relief from all the cheese, meat, and bread of the meal. I like to think of it as a pregame for dessert, too.

I newly discovered that this is Jean's favorite dish at Thanksgiving, which is why I wanted to make sure I developed a version she liked. This meant that she was my official tester for days. One time, I made her taste it while she was already lying in bed, under the covers, half-asleep (after a full day of her own recipe tests). It was so funny watching her take that goguma-filled spoon and bite into it, before closing her eyes to go back to sleep, muttering under her breath, "God, it tastes like dessert. I love it."

"Aren't you going to brush your teeth?" I asked.

"No, I'm too tired."

1 pound goguma (Korean sweet
   potatoes)

2 tablespoons honey

2 tablespoons unsalted butter,
   at room temperature, plus
   more for the baking dish

2 tablespoons dark brown sugar

1 teaspoon ground turmeric

1 teaspoon ground cinnamon

1 teaspoon soy sauce

¼ teaspoon kosher salt

1 cup whole milk

2 large eggs

14 large marshmallows, halved
   lengthwise

SERVES 6 TO 8

1. Position racks in the top and bottom thirds of the oven and preheat the oven to 400°F.

2. Place the goguma on a sheet pan and roast on the bottom rack until tender (a fork should pierce through the flesh easily), anywhere from 40 minutes to 1 hour. Remove the sheet pan and leave the oven on, but reduce the temperature to 350°F.

3. When the goguma are cool enough to handle, peel them (the skins should slip right off) and add the flesh to a large bowl. Whisk in the honey, the 2 tablespoons butter, brown sugar, turmeric, cinnamon, soy sauce, salt, milk, and eggs until smooth.

4. Grease a 2-quart baking dish with butter. Transfer the sweet potato filling to the greased baking dish and bake on the bottom rack until set (a knife inserted into the center should come out clean), about 20 minutes.

5. Remove the baking dish from the oven and carefully arrange the marshmallow halves cut-side down all over the top of the sweet potato filling, covering as much of the surface as you can with these white "tiles."

6. Preheat the broiler and, when it's ready, place the baking dish on the rack closest to it until each marshmallow is perfectly toasted and not charred, 30 seconds to 1 minute. (Watch carefully so it doesn't burn.) Serve warm.

Judy's Empanadas

My mother got this recipe from her friend Judy, a Korean woman who immigrated to Argentina before making her way to the States. Judy's empanadas are like grown-up hot pockets, neatly packaged meals of tomato-y beef, melty cheese, hard-boiled egg, and a single olive tucked into each like in a dirty martini (which makes all the difference). Stored in the freezer, they feed the family happily throughout the holiday season.

1 tablespoon olive oil

1 pound lean ground beef

1 medium yellow onion, diced

Kosher salt and freshly ground black pepper

1 (15-ounce) can tomato sauce

10 store-bought empanada wrappers (see Note)

2 large hard-boiled eggs, roughly chopped

10 pimiento-stuffed green olives

16 ounces shredded low-moisture mozzarella cheese (about 4 cups)

Vegetable oil, for frying

MAKES 10 EMPANADAS

Note You can find empanada wrappers in the frozen section of most groceries, especially Latin supermarkets. Our favorite is the orange annatto-dyed discos (they're chewier than their white counterparts).

Tip For any you don't fry and eat right away, individually wrap them in plastic and place in the freezer; thaw in the refrigerator before frying.

1. In a large skillet, heat the olive oil over high heat. Add the ground beef and cook, stirring often, until browned, 5 to 7 minutes. Stir in the onion and sauté until translucent, about 5 minutes. Season with salt and pepper, add the tomato sauce, and cook over medium-low heat for about 20 minutes, stirring occasionally. Let the filling cool completely before assembling the empanadas.

2. To assemble the empanadas, spoon a heaping tablespoon of filling into the center of a wrapper, making sure not to overstuff it or else the empanada will be difficult to seal. Top with some hard-boiled egg, a single olive, and a generous sprinkle of mozzarella. Using your finger, moisten the outer edge of the wrapper with water. Fold the wrapper in half so you have a half-moon shape. Pinch the edges of the wrapper together with your thumb and index finger to seal in the filling.

3. To finish, crimp with a fork, or try my mother's more elegant design: With your thumb, pinch a small section of the edge over into the dough and repeat all around so you're left with a sequence of rounded rainbows (see photo).

4. To fry the empanadas, pour about 2 inches vegetable oil into a medium pot. Heat over medium-high heat until it reaches 350°F on an instant-read thermometer.

5. Line a plate with paper towels. Working in batches of one or two, add the empanadas to the hot oil and deep-fry, turning them often with a frying spider or slotted spoon, until golden brown on both sides, about 5 minutes total. Transfer to the paper towels to drain. Although the fried empanadas will last up to 2 days in the refrigerator, they're best eaten hot and fresh.

Lasagna
with Gochugaru Oil

Nothing about lasagna is especially *hard*. It just takes a few steps (i.e., time). One major thing that has made homemade lasagna so much easier and more manageable, in my opinion, is cutting out the lasagna boiling step. You could use no-boil noodles, but they're thinner and less chewy than regular ones, not to mention they usually don't have the ruffles— and those ruffles are so delicious texturally. I learned from Ned in the comments section of Samin Nosrat's "The Big Lasagna Recipe" in *The New York Times* that you can soak regular dried lasagna noodles in hot water for a few minutes and they'll become pliable enough to bake. This method makes so much sense because then your noodles maintain their texture, especially once slathered in sauce and baked in the oven for an hour (thanks, Ned!).

Lasagna is a really wonderful way to feed a lot of people one big delicious thing at once. The base sauce starts off à la Marcella Hazan, the Italian food writer, with an onion (here, red) and butter (a whole stick). Both ingredients transform the tomatoes, adding mellowness, where all the punchy additions, gochujang and anchovies, add richness and so much umami. The gochugaru is key, though: As the gochugaru cooks down with the rest of the ingredients, but especially with the butter, it forms its own chile oil that floats deliciously on top of the sauce and even over the cheese in the final lasagna. Its flavor is red, hot, and full of sweet, aromatic flavor.

I might serve this lasagna with a side salad of crunchy romaine, raw red onions, balsamic vinegar, olive oil, and lots of freshly ground black pepper. I don't know why, but raw red onions and balsamic vinegar always take me back to another time and place, i.e., Macaroni Grill in the '90s.

RECIPE CONTINUES

FOR THE TOMATO SAUCE

1 (28-ounce) can whole peeled tomatoes, preferably San Marzano

1 stick (½ cup) unsalted butter

1 large red onion, diced

2 tablespoons sugar

1 teaspoon dried oregano

1 teaspoon kosher salt, plus more to taste

Freshly ground black pepper

3 tablespoons gochugaru

1 tablespoon gochujang

1 (2-ounce) tin anchovy fillets

FOR THE CHEESE FILLING

1 pound fresh ricotta cheese

1 cup shredded mozzarella cheese, plus more for the top

1 cup grated Parmesan cheese, plus more for the top

½ cup heavy cream

1 large egg

10 ounces frozen chopped spinach, thawed and squeezed to remove excess moisture

Kosher salt and freshly ground black pepper

FOR THE LASAGNA

1 pound lasagna noodles

MAKES ONE 9 × 13-INCH LASAGNA

1. Make the tomato sauce: In a large Dutch oven, combine the tomatoes, butter, onion, sugar, oregano, salt, black pepper to taste, gochugaru, gochujang, and anchovies. Bring to a boil over medium-high heat, stirring occasionally, then reduce to a gentle simmer and cook, uncovered, until the sauce is thick and jammy, about 45 minutes.

2. Meanwhile, make the cheese filling: In a medium bowl, stir together the ricotta, mozzarella, Parmesan, cream, egg, and spinach. Season with salt and pepper and set aside.

3. "Cook" the lasagna noodles: Fill a 9 × 13-inch baking pan with recently boiled water from a pot or kettle. Add the lasagna noodles to the hot water, letting them soften and making sure to turn them every couple of minutes so they don't stick to each other, about 5 minutes. Drain and set aside. Dry out the pan with a kitchen towel.

4. Preheat the oven to 350°F.

5. Assemble the lasagna: Transfer the slightly cooled tomato sauce to a food processor or blender and puree until smooth. In the baking pan, spread one-quarter of the sauce on the bottom and put down a layer of noodles, breaking one or two accordingly to create a complete layer. Top with half of the cheese filling. Repeat these layers once, topping with a final layer of noodles and the remaining sauce. Shower the top with more mozzarella cheese and a little Parm. Cover the lasagna with foil.

6. Bake the lasagna, covered, until warmed through and bubbling, about 40 minutes. Remove the foil and bake just until the cheese on top is melty but not too browned, 15 to 20 minutes. Let sit to cool slightly before cutting and serving.

Roasted Bo Ssam
with Coffee, Garlic, and Bay Leaves

I can't tell you how many bo ssam recipes I've tried out to get to this one. I wanted a bo ssam that represents the original dish—ordinarily a pork belly boiled in an aromatic potion flavored with doenjang—but something I could call my own. Not that this is entirely my own. It draws inspiration from a Nigella Lawson recipe of pork loin with bay leaves; that dish taught me what bay leaves actually taste like: woodsy and indelibly savory. The result is a wonderfully juicy, garlicky, black peppery piece of meat that lingers on your tongue with umami for miles. Pork belly gets the same treatment here, but with coffee, ginger, and bay, flavors commonly added to the cauldron of water used to boil bo ssam. Roasting it gets you a nice char on the outside and lets you concentrate those bo ssam flavors rather than having them seep into the liquid.

You can serve your roast with anything. Salted napa cabbage, fresh raw oysters, and radish salad would be traditional. But here I have a spring version with lots of lettuces and a bright, balanced soy sauce and onion condiment that pairs beautifully with the pork.

FOR THE ROASTED BO SSAM

- 1 teaspoon coarsely ground coffee
- 4 large garlic cloves, peeled
- 1-inch piece fresh ginger, roughly chopped
- 7 bay leaves, crushed into small pieces
- 2 tablespoons olive oil
- 1 teaspoon kosher salt
- 1 teaspoon freshly ground black pepper
- ½ teaspoon sugar
- 1¼ pounds thick-cut, boneless pork belly slab, skin removed

FOR THE SOY-SAUCED ONIONS

- 1½ tablespoons soy sauce
- 2 tablespoons rice vinegar
- 2 tablespoons sugar
- ½ tablespoon wasabi paste
- ½ yellow onion, thinly sliced

FOR THE SSAMJANG

- 1 tablespoon doenjang (see page 23)
- 2 teaspoons toasted sesame oil
- ½ teaspoon dark brown sugar
- 1 large garlic clove, finely grated
- 1 large scallion, thinly sliced on the diagonal
- Freshly ground black pepper

FOR SERVING

- 2 large garlic cloves, thinly sliced
- Saeujeot (salted fermented shrimp; see page 25)
- Cooked white rice (page 128)
- Various salad leaves, such as perilla, red leaf lettuce, romaine, and radicchio, for wrapping

SERVES 4 TO 6

RECIPE CONTINUES

1. Make the bo ssam: In a mortar and pestle (or using a food processor, preferably one with a small bowl attachment), pound the coffee, garlic cloves, ginger, and bay leaves into a paste. Stir in the olive oil, salt, pepper, and sugar. Smear this aromatic paste all over the pork, cover, and marinate in the fridge overnight or up to 24 hours. (You can also just roast it right away—it'll still taste great.)

2. When ready to cook, preheat the oven to 450°F. If the pork has been refrigerated, let it sit out at room temperature for 30 minutes.

3. Place the bo ssam on a sheet pan and roast until the outsides are caramelized and the edges are slightly charred, about 30 minutes. Remove from the oven and transfer to a cutting board. Set aside to rest for about 10 minutes while you prepare the soy-sauced onions and dipping sauce.

4. Make the soy-sauced onions: In a medium bowl, whisk together 2 tablespoons water, the soy sauce, vinegar, sugar, and wasabi. Toss the sliced onion in the dressing, plate it, and set aside.

5. Make the ssamjang: In a small bowl, stir together the doenjang, sesame oil, brown sugar, garlic, and scallion. Season with black pepper. Transfer to a small serving dish and set aside.

6. To serve: Slice the bo ssam as thinly as you can and arrange on a platter. Set the garlic slices and salted fermented shrimp in separate small dishes to serve alongside the bo ssam with the soy-sauced onions, the ssamjang, the rice, and all of the salad leaves.

Sheet-Pan Japchae
with Roasted Wild Mushrooms

In my family, when we're having japchae, we always seem to pick out and eat the mushrooms first, so I figured: Why not just develop a version with only mushrooms? I found that roasting a bunch of different varieties at once on a sheet pan to get them nice and crispy means you can simultaneously boil some noodles and prepare the dressing on the side. As with many sheet-pan recipes, this is a great way to make a lot of one thing at once, which is ideal for parties (perfect since japchae is peak party food). The cooking here is short and easy, meaning the eating can be long and leisurely. I love this kind of recipe: one very flavorful thing going in the oven (in this case, the medley of roasted mushrooms), a base carbohydrate (hey, sweet potato noodles) boiling on the stove, and a simple sauce a-stirring away (looking at you, soy sauce, garlic, and brown sugar). All three components get tossed together at the end, and you're done.

8 ounces dried dangmyeon (sweet potato noodles)

1 pound wild mushrooms, such as oyster, shiitake (stems removed), and chanterelle, torn into bite-size pieces

5 large scallions, cut into 3-inch lengths

Olive oil

Kosher salt and freshly ground black pepper

2 tablespoons plus 1 teaspoon soy sauce

1 tablespoon toasted sesame oil

1 tablespoon dark brown sugar

1 tablespoon maple syrup

1 large garlic clove, finely grated

Toasted sesame seeds, for serving

SERVES 4 TO 6

1. Position a rack as close to the broiler element as possible and preheat the broiler.

2. Bring a large pot of water to a boil and cook the dangmyeon according to package directions.

3. Meanwhile, arrange the mushrooms and scallions on a sheet pan and toss with some olive oil. Place under the broiler and roast until deeply caramelized and crispy, about 5 minutes. Watch them carefully. Remove the pan from the oven and season with salt and pepper.

4. In a small bowl, whisk together the soy sauce, sesame oil, brown sugar, maple syrup, and garlic. When the noodles are done cooking, drain them and add them directly to the sheet pan with the roasted mushrooms. Pour the dressing over the noodles and toss everything together with tongs.

5. To serve, transfer the japchae to a large platter and sprinkle with sesame seeds.

Sheet-Pan LA Kalbi
with Sprite

Though you could make the marinade for these short ribs without a food processor, I highly recommend using one, as it really helps to break down the fibers of the pear, garlic, and ginger. That trick plus Jean's latest addition to her decades-old kalbi recipe, Sprite—a surprise ingredient, even for me—gives this some fun novelty factor (though adding sugary sodas to Korean marinades is actually quite common these days). "It means you can use less sugar," she told me, "but the Sprite also adds moisture."

I love cooking these ribs for dinner parties because the recipe almost begs that you prep it ahead of time: An overnight soak in the garlicky, gingery, soy sauce–laden marinade makes for the most flavorful barbecue. Even better if they can sit to marinate for two to three days. I use the term "barbecue" here loosely, as these ribs cook from start to finish on a sheet pan versus on the grill, which means significantly less splatter—but they still have all the charred, caramelized wonder of the fire. One final bit of advice: Do yourself a favor and line your sheet pan with parchment paper. I learned the hard way.

½ large Korean pear (aka Asian pear), cored (about 8 ounces)

10 large garlic cloves, peeled

2-inch piece fresh ginger

½ cup Sprite

¼ cup soy sauce

¼ cup mirim

2 tablespoons dark brown sugar

2 tablespoons toasted sesame oil

Freshly ground black pepper

2 pounds ¼-inch-thick flanken-cut beef short ribs (LA-style kalbi)

2 large scallions, thinly sliced on the diagonal, for garnish

Cooked white rice (page 128), for serving

SERVES 4 TO 6

1. In a food processor, blitz together the pear, garlic, ginger, Sprite, soy sauce, mirim, brown sugar, and sesame oil until smooth. Season generously with black pepper.

2. Rinse the short ribs under cold tap water to get rid of any bone fragments and pat them dry. Place them in a resealable container and pour over the marinade, shmooshing (technical term) them around so they're evenly coated. Cover and marinate in the fridge for 4 hours or up to overnight.

3. When ready to cook, preheat the oven to 450°F. Line a sheet pan with parchment paper.

4. Drain the short ribs in a colander over the sink, then arrange them on the lined pan. Roast until the ribs caramelize at the edges, about 30 minutes.

5. Remove from the oven and garnish with scallions. Serve with white rice.

Salt-and-Pepper Ribs
with Fresh Mint Sauce

These ribs are actually my dad's "recipe": seasoned with just salt and pepper. You'll be surprised at how good they are with so few adornments. He usually grills them, which gives them a nice char, but I found that I could roast them on a sheet pan at a high temperature and achieve a similar result with less work (plus, now I can make them in NYC, where I don't have outdoor space—or a grill). Because the ribs are so simple, the mint sauce really helps pick everything up with its fresh, sweet, vinegary brightness. I made these for friends one summer evening, and watched with pride and happiness as they absolutely polished them off, basically lapping up the sauce and licking the platter clean. All that was remaining at the end of dinner was a pile of pork bones in the middle of the table. Now I know how my dad feels.

FOR THE RIBS

2 racks baby back ribs (2 to 3 pounds), cut into individual ribs

2 tablespoons olive oil

Kosher salt and freshly ground black pepper

FOR THE FRESH MINT SAUCE

4 cups fresh mint, roughly chopped

¼ cup rice vinegar, plus more to taste

2 teaspoons sugar, plus more to taste

1 teaspoon kosher salt, plus more to taste

FOR SERVING

Fresh mint leaves, larger leaves torn

Cooked white rice (page 128)

SERVES 4 TO 6

1. Preheat the oven to 450°F.

2. Make the ribs: Place the ribs on a sheet pan and drizzle with the olive oil. Season with salt and lots of pepper and toss with your hands to coat. Roast until the ribs are cooked through and slightly charred, 20 to 30 minutes.

3. Meanwhile, make the fresh mint sauce: In a medium bowl, stir together the mint, ¼ cup water, the vinegar, sugar, and salt. Taste and adjust for seasoning: Does it need more sharpness? Add vinegar. More sweetness? Sugar. More salt? You get the drill.

4. To serve: Transfer the ribs to a large platter and strew with some fresh mint leaves. Serve with the white rice and the fresh mint sauce alongside, letting guests spoon it over their plates.

Microwave Gyeranjjim
with Chicken Broth

My favorite thing at Korean barbecue restaurants is actually not the meat, but the bubbling cauldron of custardy, molten egg often served as a banchan with the protein. The secret to a good gyeranjjim is the broth, and the ratio of egg to water. I love using chicken broth because it's what I always have lying around, not least because some of it gets left over at the end, and it's incredibly soul-soothing to chase the custardy, savory egg with chicken soup. It's the breakfast of champions, though growing up my grandma would stir this into fluffy white rice stained with soy. Oh, and did you know that you can make this entirely in the microwave?

2 large eggs

1 cup chicken broth (preferably made from Better Than Bouillon base)

1 to 2 teaspoons fish sauce

1 large scallion, thinly sliced on the diagonal

SERVES 2

In a medium microwave-safe soup bowl, whisk the eggs, chicken broth, and fish sauce until well combined. Top the egg mixture with the scallion and microwave on high until the eggs have set (they'll bubble up and gain volume as they steam), anywhere from 3 to 7 minutes depending on your microwave. For this one, you really do need to serve immediately.

Aunt Georgia's Soy Sauce Fried Chicken
with Jalapeños

My Aunt Georgia's fried chicken is unmatched. I love how simple her recipe is, and within its simplicity—the careful combination of garlic, jalapeños, brown sugar, and soy sauce—lies great complexity. Her chicken stays crunchy for hours, thanks to the potato starch coating and the double fry, not to mention the savory, spicy glaze that candies the outsides. For balance, be sure to have this with the Somaek (page 243) and the Chicken Radishes (page 184).

1 whole chicken
(3 to 3½ pounds), cut
into 10 serving pieces

Kosher salt and freshly ground
black pepper

2 cups potato starch

Vegetable oil

7 large garlic cloves, thinly sliced

3 large jalapeños, thinly sliced

¼ cup packed dark brown sugar

¼ cup soy sauce

SERVES 6 TO 8

1. In a large bowl or resealable plastic bag, add the chicken pieces and season with salt and pepper. Add 1 cup of the potato starch and toss to coat each piece. Remove the chicken pieces and repeat. Add the pieces to the bowl or bag, sprinkle in the remaining 1 cup potato starch and toss to coat each piece again. Set aside on a plate until the starch on the chicken begins to look wet, about 15 minutes.

2. Pour 2 inches oil (enough to cover the chicken pieces while frying) into a large Dutch oven. Heat over medium-high heat to 350°F.

3. Line a plate with paper towels. Working in batches of a few pieces at a time, add the chicken to the hot oil and fry until lightly golden, about 4 minutes per batch. Transfer the fried

chicken to the paper towels. Then, fry these same pieces a second time until golden brown, about 8 minutes per batch. Set these twice-fried chicken pieces aside on a wire rack until you've double-fried all of the chicken.

4. In a medium skillet, combine ½ cup vegetable oil, the garlic, 2 of the jalapeños, the brown sugar, and soy sauce and set over medium-high heat until it bubbles up. Add a few pieces of the fried chicken to the sauce and use tongs to quickly turn them over in the glaze just until coated. Remove and transfer to a serving platter. Repeat with the remaining chicken.

5. Garnish the fried chicken with the remaining jalapeño slices and serve immediately or at room temperature, when the soy sauce glaze on the outside will be at its crunchiest.

Crispy Lemon-Pepper Bulgogi
with Quick-Pickled Shallots

What I have here is not the comforting, melt-in-your-mouth bulgogi—thinly sliced beef, marinated then grilled—that's so ubiquitous in Korean restaurants and most home kitchens today. This is my own creation, adding to the pantheon of bulgogi recipes out there. As a nod to my hometown (lemon pepper has a deep and passionate fan base in Atlanta), the citrusy, aromatic spice rub in this version dusts thinly sliced rib eye, which gets seared and then marinated post-cook in a lemony shallot mixture. The thing with a beef cut this thin is you want to fry it on a very hot surface for as little time as possible (but while also gaining as much color in that short time). It's a dance and one that is best done on a grill pan, but a very hot skillet would work, too. You want crisp edges, and if you're lucky, for the fat to bubble up and crisp.

On the subject of black pepper: I'm convinced that we as home cooks don't use as much of it as we could, and don't truly know what it even tastes like. One proper lick and you can appreciate the peppercorn for what it really is: an aromatic berry. Couple that fruitiness with dehydrated lemon zest (it takes just 20 minutes in the oven), which, when rubbed into the coarse black pepper, releases its oils and latches onto the pepper, and vice versa, and they seem almost to transform one another. All that pepper will give you a tingling sensation, as well, and tastes fab with the sour-sweet quick-pickled shallots.

Grated zest and juice of 1 large lemon

2 shallots, thinly sliced

Kosher salt

1 tablespoon black peppercorns

1 teaspoon demerara sugar (such as Sugar in the Raw)

½ teaspoon garlic powder

1 pound thinly sliced rib eye (or other meat for bulgogi-style dishes; see Tip, page 242)

Vegetable oil

1 jalapeño, thinly sliced into rings

Fresh cilantro leaves plus tender stems, lots of it

Cooked white rice (page 128), for serving

SERVES 4

1. Preheat the oven to 170°F.

2. Evenly spread out the lemon zest on a sheet pan and bake until completely dried out, 20 to 30 minutes.

3. Meanwhile, mix the lemon juice and shallots in a small bowl, season with salt, toss, and set aside to quick-pickle.

RECIPE CONTINUES

4. Add the dried-out lemon zest and the black peppercorns to a spice grinder or mortar/pestle and grind until coarse. Transfer to a small bowl and stir in 1 teaspoon salt, the demerara sugar, and garlic powder.

5. Use a paper towel to pat the meat dry and lay it out on a cutting board or sheet pan in a single layer. Season both sides with the lemon pepper.

6. Heat a large grill pan or skillet until very, very hot (you may see a wisp of smoke rise from the surface) and add enough oil to lightly coat the bottom. Add the bulgogi to the pan in a single layer and cook until crispy and well browned, about 1 minute on the first side and literally a few seconds on the second. You may need to work in batches so as not to overcrowd the pan. Transfer to a plate and top with the pickled shallots, jalapeño, and cilantro. Serve with white rice.

Sheet-Pan Version

Instead of pan-searing, you could actually drizzle some oil over the meat and broil it on the top rack until crispy and well browned, 2 to 3 minutes (just watch it carefully so it doesn't burn). This will only work with broilers that run very hot—if you suspect yours doesn't, then stick to the pan-searing method in the recipe.

Tip If you can't find bulgogi-style beef, then you can just do it yourself: Place a boneless rib eye in the freezer for a few minutes to firm up, then slice thinly with a very sharp knife.

Two Soju Cocktails

Soju, a clear spirit traditionally made from rice (though modern bottles primarily use potato and sweet potato), is one of the mainstays of Korean drinking culture. And its versatility is unmatchable. My dad's favorite way of drinking it is over lots of ice with lime juice—not fresh, the reconstituted kind from the green plastic lime bottle. The virtue of soju lies in its mild, gently sweet taste, which makes it perfect for cocktails.

Somaek

Somaek is just a portmanteau of the words *soju* and *maekju*, or beer. My brother Kevin is the somaek expert in this family. According to him, not all somaeks are made the same; some are better than others. I never understood somaek culture until I started making them for myself and realized how wonderful and refreshing they can be, especially with fried chicken (page 239). One key point: The type of beer *matters*. A Korean brand like Kloud is silky smooth with a nice foam, and lighter beers like Hite and Cass are crisp, clean, and classic; both work nicely with soju. If you can't find them, look for a Pilsner-style beer with a crisp, refreshing taste. The ratio of soju to beer is also key, though it can vary depending on personal taste. The golden ratio, according to Kevin, is 3 parts soju to 7 parts maek. I agree. Here's why it works: The soju's sweetness balances the bitterness of the beer, and the beer offsets any alcoholic bite of the soju. The result? A supremely balanced (and ahem, surprisingly alcoholic) drink that is greater than the sum of its parts.

3½ ounces light Korean beer, such as Kloud, Cass, or Hite

1½ ounces soju

MAKES 1 COCKTAIL

Fill a small glass with the beer. Add the soju and, using a spoon, mix the two together to create a foamy top. You want this foamy top because it tastes like a cloud.

RECIPE CONTINUES

Clementine 50/50

One of my favorite bars in New York City had a bar manager named Rustun, who mixed up some of the most wonderful drinks. I really miss him. Before he moved away during the pandemic, he taught me that a vodka martini doesn't have to punch you in the face with alcohol; instead, it can float on the tongue, make you hungry. I mix half soju and half dry vermouth with a splash of fresh clementine juice that adds balance, but not too much sweetness. If clementines aren't in season, then you can replace it with another citrus juice, such as lemon, grapefruit, or nothing at all.

Ice
1½ ounces soju
1½ ounces dry vermouth
1 clementine

MAKES 1 COCKTAIL

1. Fill a tall glass (like a pint glass or tumbler) with ice and add the soju and vermouth. Use a vegetable peeler to shave off a long, thin strip of clementine peel. Cut the clementine in half and juice it into the glass. Using a long spoon, stir the ice in a circular motion to chill the drink. Strain it into a martini glass or coupe.

2. With the orange side of the peel facing the martini glass or coupe, squeeze it in half to release the oils into the drink and then rub the orange side against the lip of the glass. Twist the peel and add it to the drink or hang it on the lip of the glass.

Korean Bakery

Baked weekend projects

Back in her college days in Busan, South Korea, a ballet major named Seung Hee Kim frequented a bakery downtown called White Windmill. It was her favorite place to stop in for a cup of coffee and bread between classes. Years later, Ms. Kim, herself the daughter of a bakery owner, would immigrate to Atlanta and open up her own shop on Buford Highway. She would call the new business White Windmill, promising to serve up loaves as light and as effervescent as the ones from her hometown. And she delivered. White Windmill, which now has three stores in and around Atlanta, is known for baking up some of the city's best Korean pastries: fluffy white milk breads, chewy black sesame rolls, and fresh cream cakes bejeweled with glossy strawberries.

Today, everyone in the Atlanta Korean community knows Ms. Kim. She's famous in a "My mom is friends with her" kind of way. Even Jean has Ms. Kim's number saved in her phone. All this goes to say that the White Windmill lady is *très* cool. You can often find her at the flagship store on Buford Highway, which opened in 2002, maybe making a customer's latte or roasting beans (White Windmill is also famous for coffee, being one of the first spots in the area to freshly roast beans). Even though she's the boss, Ms. Kim is always there with her employees, greeting customers and checking on the store. The menu changes often, too, which is probably why business is so good.

White Windmill was a big part of my life growing up, so I remember it well. It's equidistant from my parents' church (where I led the youth group praise band from eighth grade to senior year of high school), the music academy (where I took flute lessons from a wonderful man named Kelly, and also where my mother first asked me, "Are you gay?"), and my dad's store (where he's sold cell phones and cell phone accessories since the early 1990s). You could say it's a cultural nexus for Korean Americans in Atlanta. I drove by that bakery every single day of my life until I moved to New York and only now realize how much I took it for granted. My whole childhood I thought it was just another bakery chain flown in from Korea. But this woman, Ms. Kim, created a safe space for Korean immigrants like my parents to come and go as they please—to buy their bread, pastries, and birthday cakes from a Korean-owned business, sure, but also to meet with friends, to go on dates, and to run into other Koreans who had the same idea to stop in for a quick coffee on a Sunday afternoon. If you're taking a seat at a Korean bakery, chances are you're there to linger. You could sit there for hours and no one would bother you or ask you to leave. Even more, everyone speaks Korean.

My mother recalls how, back in the 1980s, when they first arrived in America, there really weren't many Korean gathering spaces like this. You'd take your kids to McDonald's for lunch and hope to run into another Korean mom in the ball pit. In this way, I've always felt that Korean bakeries like White Windmill were so much more than just a regular spot to get your milk bread; it was one of the first and most essential meeting points for a growing community of Korean immigrants in Atlanta. As this community slowly migrated out to the suburbs, Korean bakeries also started popping up there, including a couple more White Windmills.

It's telling that all of these bakeries are named after European-sounding things like Paris Baguette, Tous les Jours, and Mozart. Walking into any one of these stores often feels like you've just stepped into a utopian dreamland, a sugary and very Korean interpretation of what a bakery in a small town in the Alps might look like. Taking inspiration from French technique and using Asian ingredients (and catering to Korean palates), the desserts you'll find in these bakeries are often less sweet than American baked goods, or even French ones, for that matter. You'll find a lot of red bean, green tea, mocha, black sesame, and fruit-filled treats that delight and surprise every time.

In many Korean American households, cut fruit is the most common after-dinner snack—the go-to home "dessert," if you will. But I wanted to offer some recipes that pay homage to the myriad sweet joys of bakeries like Ms. Kim's. You won't find exact replicas of those perfectly plastic-wrapped treats here. What you will find are the kinds of rustic, light weekend baking projects that are absorbing but not demanding, like the Milk Bread with Maple Syrup (page 251) that opens the chapter, the Chewy Black Sesame Rice Cake (page 268) that pays homage to those Korean bakery mochi rolls (my personal favorite), and the Whipped Cream Snacking Cake with Fresh Fruit (page 270), my much lazier, single-layer take on the iconic fresh cream cakes that line the glass cases of Ms. Kim's bakery.

Milk Bread
with Maple Syrup

This sikbbang is the bread my mother would buy from the Korean bakery, the soft loaf from which she would then make my packed lunches in grade school: ham and mayo sandwiches, always. The bread felt like feathers in my mouth in between creamy bayous of mayonnaise and cool, salty panels of ham.

There was a point during the pandemic when I would make a loaf every day. It became a ritual—bread church. Every night, instead of writing my manuscript, I would go downstairs and bake one of these loaves, each time tweaking one little thing. I would swap some of the sugar for honey, then that honey for maple syrup. I would then increase the maple syrup four times because the family loved the flavor and wanted more of it. I would alternate between all-purpose and bread flour, ultimately landing on the latter's chew. I would try different levels of yeast, and different combinations of milk, cream, and butter. Egg yolks, egg whites, and whole eggs. Machine versus no machine.

The number one secret about bread baking that no one tells you is how easy it can be. In the case of milk bread, for instance, it's not particularly hard to make the roux "starter" called tangzhong, which is just a slurry of liquid (in this case, milk) and flour (in this case, bread flour) that gets cooked before adding the rest of the ingredients. (In case you're wondering: The tangzhong helps the dough absorb the rest of the flour it's about to get, all four cups of it.) It's actually pretty chill when you're building your dough straight in the pot with the roux: first some cream (my little trick to cool down the hot starter and to add fat—I prefer this to butter), bread flour (which has more protein and thus more chew than all-purpose), maple syrup (for milk bread's characteristic sweetness, and for that brown tree-bark flavor), salt (for balance), and of course yeast (added last atop the cooler ingredients so as not to risk killing any of the cultures with heat). This dough comes together in just 5 minutes. It couldn't be easier.

It's the waiting that takes a bit. At first the dough will be very wet and sticky, almost like a drop biscuit. You'll need to rest this for 1 hour after mixing it, then knead it—by hand, no stand mixer necessary—for just 5 minutes. In those 5 minutes, and with the help of a small ½ cup of

RECIPE CONTINUES

"insurance" flour, the dough will come together into a soft, voluptuous ball that smells of raw dough and amber maple. Then comes my favorite bit: dividing the one big ball into two smaller balls, both of which get nestled side by side into a greased loaf pan, covered with a damp kitchen towel, and left alone to proof again for another hour. I call this stage the butt stage (because it looks like a butt). It never stops sparking joy to come back after 60 minutes to find that my bread butt has doubled in size.

But the true joy of baking a fresh loaf of milk bread at home is doing it alone, in the quiet of my evening. If I'm making bread, it's likely because my mind is buzzing, and I need to busy my hands. When my hands are kneading bread, I can turn off my brain for a couple hours (the total time it takes to wait for this dough to rest). In those two essential hours, I give myself one rule: No thinking. The reward for my idleness? Opening the oven door to let out that fresh-baked-bread smell, a yeasty sweetness that reminds me of all the Korean bakeries lining Buford Highway, my childhood home with the peach tree in the front yard, and beyond.

FOR THE TANGZHONG
½ cup (72 grams) bread flour
1 cup whole milk

FOR THE BREAD
½ cup heavy cream
4 cups (576 grams) bread flour, plus ½ cup (72 grams) to roll out
1 cup maple syrup
1 large egg
1½ teaspoons kosher salt
4½ teaspoons (14 grams) active dry yeast (2 envelopes)
Cooking spray

MAKES 1 LOAF

1. Make the tangzhong: In a medium pot, whisk together the bread flour and milk until relatively smooth. Set over medium-low heat and cook, whisking constantly, until the mixture thickens into a texture not unlike mashed potatoes or grits, 2 to 3 minutes. You may see lumps at first, but as you continue to whisk and the flour cooks, your mixture will smooth out.

2. Make the bread: Remove the pot from the heat and whisk in the cream until smooth, which will cool down the mixture and add some necessary fat. To the creamy mixture, add 4 cups (576 grams) of the bread flour, the maple syrup, egg, salt, and yeast and stir with a wooden spoon or rubber spatula until well combined and you can no longer see any streaks of egg or flour. Cover the pot with a lid and let sit in a warm place to proof and hydrate until doubled in size, about 1 hour.

3. Keep the remaining ½ cup (72 grams) bread flour next to you for this kneading step: Dust a clean surface, such as a kitchen counter or large wood cutting board, with some of the flour and turn the dough out onto the surface. Dust some more flour on top of the dough and on your hands, and knead the dough into a ball using both hands. As you start to feel the dough get sticky, add more of the flour. The goal here is to not use more than that ½ cup of flour to knead the dough and at the same time develop enough gluten in it so that it's no longer sticky, 5 to 7 minutes.

4. When the dough starts to feel less and less sticky under your hands, you can cut the dough in half with a knife, then flatten each piece using your hands, pulling the corners of each piece up and over the center, all around, so that you're creating two tight balls. Twist the pulled-up edges to seal and turn the balls over so their smooth sides are facing up. Grease a 9 × 5-inch loaf pan with cooking spray. Nestle the two balls side by side in the pan and let sit, covered, in a warm place in your kitchen until doubled in size again, 1 to 1½ hours. This is the second and last proof.

5. Preheat the oven to 350°F.

6. Bake the bread until the crust is dark brown and an instant-read thermometer inserted in the center reads 190°F, about 40 minutes.

7. Remove from the oven and let cool slightly in the pan before taking the bread out and slicing into it. (Technically you should cool it completely before eating, but come on: Even I won't bar you from the glorious experience of tearing into a fresh, warm loaf of sweet milk bread. There's nothing like it.) The bread will keep for up to 3 to 4 days in a closed container at room temperature.

A Proper Grilled Cheese

One of the best things you can make with fresh homemade milk bread is a grilled cheese sandwich. The bread is slightly sweet because of the maple syrup in the dough, and I love that sweetness alongside as much shredded mozzarella as I can pile between the two slices (usually about ½ cup). Some of the cheese will fall out of the sandwich and into the pan and caramelize around the edges of the bread as it grills in a soft panel of foamy butter. And if you slather mayo on the inside *before* adding the cheese, it will almost meld with the cheese so you have a comfortingly bland, gooey, stretchy toasted sandwich that tastes not unlike a mozzarella in carrozza (but without the breading).

Honeyed Biscuits
with Strawberry Refrigerator Jam

When my father first landed in America in 1983, the first thing he ate was a KFC biscuit. All he remembers is that it was very buttery. My mom chimed in from across the table, "Korea has really good KFC, actually." "No, this was in America," my dad corrected her. Turns out the first KFC arrived in Korea in 1984, a year after my dad moved to America and had his first biscuit. The thing is, perhaps ironically, I ate a KFC biscuit like that, too—but in Korea. The *Korean* KFC biscuit tasted, as my dad described the American one, buttery, but it was also caramelized on the outside, almost brûléed or candied like the crust of a good kouign-amann (though this is nothing as fancy as that).

I love this recipe, my take on that KFC biscuit, because there's no kneading or cutting or rolling out. There's just a bowl, a spoon, and an ice cream scoop for truly excellent drop biscuits. And though you could just serve this with store-bought strawberry jam, you'll see from the way I do it that making your own really isn't very hard at all. The only condition is that this is a refrigerator jam, meaning you have to keep it in the fridge and eat it within the week (easy to do). That's due to the butter, which has a purpose: According to the USDA, a little butter stirred in at the end breaks the surface tension of the jam, letting the myriad air bubbles escape and reducing that foamy cloudiness that plagues so many homemade preserves.

FOR THE BISCUITS

2 cups (256 grams) all-purpose flour

¾ teaspoon kosher salt

2 tablespoons sugar

1 tablespoon baking powder

1 stick (½ cup) unsalted butter, cut into ¼-inch pieces

1 cup whole milk

1 tablespoon rice vinegar

1 tablespoon honey, plus more for serving

FOR THE STRAWBERRY JAM

1 pound strawberries, hulled and quartered

Grated zest and juice of 1 clementine or orange

2 cups (400 grams) sugar

Pinch of kosher salt

½ tablespoon unsalted butter

MAKES 12 BISCUITS

RECIPE CONTINUES

1. Make the biscuits: Preheat the oven to 400°F. Line a sheet pan with parchment paper.

2. In a large bowl, using your hands, stir together the flour, salt, 1 tablespoon of the sugar, and the baking powder until combined. Add the butter, squishing each butter piece in between your fingers until every single one has been (a) flattened and (b) coated in flour. This mixture should look like a loose, gravelly sand that's been slightly dampened by ocean water.

3. Add the milk and rice vinegar and stir with a wooden spoon until just combined; it should look like a nubbly muffin batter. Using a medium ice cream scoop, portion out 12 biscuits, evenly spacing them out on the pan. Drizzle the tops with the honey and sprinkle with the remaining 1 tablespoon sugar.

4. Bake until the tops of the biscuits are golden and the edges crispy, about 20 minutes.

5. Meanwhile, make the strawberry jam: In a large pot, combine the strawberries, clementine zest, clementine juice, sugar, and salt and bring to a gentle boil over medium heat. Reduce the heat to low and cook, stirring occasionally, until the fruit breaks down, the mixture reduces significantly,

and the juices are thickened and syrupy, 35 to 40 minutes. Remove from the heat and stir in the butter. Let the jam cool slightly. (Store leftovers in the refrigerator and eat within the week.)

6. Serve the biscuits while warm with a drizzle of extra honey either on the side or on top, as well as with the fresh jam.

The author's father, Ki, posing in Atlanta's Hartsfield-Jackson International Airport in 1983.

Korean Pear Galette
with Salted Cinnamon Whipped Cream

When I came out to my parents, I was dating a boy who lived in Atlanta. Every time I drove down to see him, my mom would give me food to bring over to my "friend" (what she called him). The usual suspects, you know: Tupperwares of kimchi fried rice (page 136), frozen Argentine empanadas (page 222) from Christmas, and Korean pears—the fancy ones wrapped in Styrofoam lace so they don't bruise on their way to the Korean grocery store, or to a boy's house. Though I never asked her about this, the gesture felt significant to me. It was her way of saying, "I'm happy you have someone," even if at the moment she was still working through her feelings about my sexuality and couldn't say the words namja chingu ("boyfriend" in Korean).

One night, my "friend" made a galette out of one of Jean's pears. Suddenly this familiar thing, this crisp Korean pear—which I always ate raw, peeled, and cut with the steel blade of my mother's paring knife— was a full-fledged pie. He even shingled the pears like a merman's scales, which is where I got the idea.

Korean pears, also known as Asian pears, have the most wonderfully crisp texture, reminiscent of jicama and less grainy than their cousins Bosc and Anjou, which makes them ideal for baking. Flavorwise, Korean pears have a mild, floral sweetness that works well with aromatic spices like fresh ginger and cinnamon. Many Koreans might recognize this flavor combination in sujeonggwa, a Korean cinnamon punch that's spiked with ginger and sometimes boiled with pear.

This dessert also benefits greatly from a milder cooling element—this time in the form of a salted cinnamon whipped cream, which tastes like Cinnamon Toast Crunch. Kudos to my brother for teaching me that you can go heavy on the salt when making whipped cream. If you've never salted your cream before—like, *really* salted it—then it's never too late to start.

Recently, in the car while driving home from the store, my mother asked me, "How's your friend doing?" (referring to my new boyfriend, Paolo). Before I could answer, she caught herself and recast her question, "How's your *namja chingu* doing?" And we talked about him for the rest of the drive.

RECIPE CONTINUES

FOR THE DOUGH

1 cup (128 grams) all-purpose flour, plus more for dusting

2 tablespoons granulated sugar

½ teaspoon kosher salt

7 tablespoons cold unsalted butter, cut into ½-inch cubes

1 tablespoon rice vinegar

1 to 3 tablespoons ice water

FOR THE FILLING

1 Korean pear (aka Asian pear; 6 to 8 ounces), halved, cored, and thinly sliced into half-moons

Grated zest and juice of ½ lemon

1 teaspoon grated fresh ginger

½ teaspoon ground cinnamon

3 tablespoons dark brown sugar

1 tablespoon heavy cream

1 tablespoon demerara sugar (such as Sugar in the Raw)

Flaky sea salt

FOR THE WHIPPED CREAM

1 cup heavy cream

2 tablespoons granulated sugar

½ teaspoon ground cinnamon

¼ teaspoon kosher salt

MAKES ONE 8-INCH GALETTE

1. Make the dough: In a large bowl, using your hands, stir together the flour, granulated sugar, and salt until combined. Add the butter, squishing each butter piece in between your fingers until every single butter cube has been flattened and coated in flour. This mixture should look like a loose, gravelly soil with big pieces and small pieces and lots of flattened, flour-coated butter.

2. Add the rice vinegar and 1 tablespoon of the ice water and toss gently with your hands until the dough comes together into a single ball. You may need more ice water for this to happen, but also you might not! If you do, add it, a scant tablespoon at a time. It's all right if some parts of the dough are dry and slightly falling apart. Wrap it in a sheet of plastic wrap, then sort of squish everything together into a neat disc, and transfer to the fridge to rest for at least 2 hours or overnight. As the dough rests, it will hydrate and become much less crumbly and easier to work with.

3. When you're ready to bake the galette, preheat the oven to 400°F. Line a sheet pan with parchment paper.

4. Make the filling: In a large bowl, toss together the pear slices, lemon zest, lemon juice, ginger, cinnamon, and 2 tablespoons of the brown sugar until evenly mixed.

5. Take the rested dough out of the fridge. Lightly dust a clean surface with flour and roll the dough out into a 13-inch round that's about ⅛ inch thick. Use the rolling pin to transfer the dough to the lined sheet pan. Place the pears in the center, shingling them over one another like fish scales; save the accumulated juices in the bowl. Fold the edges of the dough over one another working around the circle (like the pleats of a skirt) so you're left with a 1- to 2-inch border over the fruit. Carefully pour the reserved juices into the center of the galette. Sprinkle the remaining 1 tablespoon brown sugar over the fruit. Brush the crust with the cream and sprinkle with the demerara sugar and a pinch of flaky sea salt.

6. Bake the galette until the crust has browned and the filling is bubbling, 35 to 45 minutes.

7. Meanwhile, make the whipped cream: In a large bowl (you can do this in a stand mixer, too), whisk together the heavy cream, granulated sugar, cinnamon, and salt until you have soft peaks.

8. Let the galette cool slightly before slicing into it and serving with the whipped cream.

No-Churn Ice Cream
with Dalgona Butterscotch Sauce

Like so many Internet trends, when whipped dalgona coffee took off, I had no idea it was "Korean" until a Korean friend of mine said the word in our mother accent: dal-go-na. *Oh*, dalgona ("It's sweet"). This was odd to me because this whipped instant coffee drink tastes nothing like actual dalgona, also known as ppopgi, a honeycomb-like Korean street candy that was popular in the 1970s and '80s, back when my parents were young. We called it ppopgi growing up, and I remember watching my dad make it by melting granulated sugar on a large metal spoon over the stovetop, then rapidly stirring baking soda into it (causing it to aerate and bubble up violently) to create that caramel-colored honeycomb dream. This image always made me laugh because no matter who you are, melting anything on a spoon over an open flame looks like you're doing drugs. (My dad does not do drugs.)

Dalgona coffee, on the other hand, was likely named after the color of the Korean candy, not necessarily the taste. It's argued that the drink went viral when the Korean actor Jung Il-woo tasted it on TV. But when the drink made its way to non-Korean audiences on the popular social media platform TikTok, the toffee part disappeared. And so I thought, what if this drink *did* taste like that wonderful burnt sugar? Alchemist, a Korean-owned coffee shop in Atlanta, started serving a "dalgona" coffee with actual dalgona pieces in it, which add a deep caramel-y flavor to the bitter coffee within. Inspired by their creation, I thought I would show you a simple dalgona-inspired butterscotch sauce I like to make to serve over my no-churn vanilla bean ice cream, which is my go-to ice cream recipe. There's a little instant coffee powder in the caramel because the combination of vanilla ice cream, coffee, and caramel is exceptional.

RECIPE CONTINUES

FOR THE ICE CREAM

2 cups heavy cream

½ cup sugar

Pinch of kosher salt

1 vanilla bean, split lengthwise

FOR THE DALGONA BUTTERSCOTCH
SAUCE

1 cup dark brown sugar

½ cup heavy cream

2 tablespoons unsalted butter

**1 teaspoon instant coffee
powder**

Flaky sea salt

**MAKES 1 QUART ICE CREAM
AND 1 CUP SAUCE**

1. Make the ice cream: In a large bowl (you can do this in a stand mixer, too), combine the heavy cream, sugar, and salt and scrape in the seeds from the vanilla pod. Whisk until the mixture is thick like whipped cream. Transfer to an airtight 1-quart container, cover, and freeze until firm, about 4 hours or overnight.

2. Meanwhile, make the dalgona butterscotch sauce: In a small saucepan, combine ¼ cup water and the brown sugar and cook over medium heat until the caramel reaches 240°F on an instant-read thermometer, 6 to 8 minutes. Remove from the heat and add the cream, butter, and instant coffee and whisk rapidly to combine. The consistency should be that of a pourable sauce.

3. Season the butterscotch with a pinch of the flaky sea salt and serve over a scoop of the vanilla ice cream, sprinkling more flaky sea salt on top if you'd like.

Note When scooping the ice cream from frozen, you'll want to remove it from the freezer to thaw for about 10 minutes before scooping (it should be creamy and aerated, not hard).

Honeydew Semifreddo

One of my favorite Korean treats growing up was Melona ice cream, also known as "melon bars." You could buy these creamy, pale-green, honeydew-flavored rectangular prisms at any Korean grocery or video store with an ice-cream freezer (back when there used to be entire Blockbuster-type businesses in Atlanta dedicated to VHS bootlegs of Korean television shows). When it comes to melon bars, the magic lies in their feathery texture, similar to kulfi, semifreddo, and commercial ice creams like chocolate fudge pops that coat the tongue with cool velvet. The feeling of a creamy thing melting in your mouth is both satisfying and refreshing, not to mention nostalgia-inducing. But one flavored with the delicate scent of honeydew? Stunningly surprising.

I love that in America, honeydew is often considered the worst aspect of a fruit cup or fruit salad, but in Korea, the flavor is celebrated. This probably has to do with the fruits themselves tasting better and sweeter, but I've found that you can capture the essence of honeydew—and everything that is inherently floral about it—when you add sugar and cream. When I was a kid, one melon bar was never enough for me, so in the spirit of making up for lost time (and never growing up), I decided to create my own homemade take on that childhood favorite in the form of this semifreddo—which is just Italian for "half cold."

8 ounces peeled, seeded honeydew melon, cut into pieces

4 large raw egg yolks (ones you feel confident about)

½ cup sugar

1 cup heavy cream

¼ teaspoon kosher salt

MAKES ONE 9 × 5-INCH LOAF

1. In a blender, puree the honeydew until smooth. You should have a little over 1 cup puree (but there's no need to measure). Spoon the puree into a fine-mesh sieve placed over a liquid measuring cup to collect the juice. Stir the pulp to release more juice. You should have about ½ cup honeydew juice. Set the melon aside to continue draining while you make everything else. (Discard the pulp when you're finished with it.)

2. Line a 9 × 5-inch loaf pan with plastic wrap, making sure there's enough hanging over the sides to cover the top later.

3. In a small pot, bring 1 inch of water to a gentle simmer over high heat. Reduce the heat to low and set a heatproof medium bowl over the simmering water (making sure the water doesn't touch the bottom of the bowl). Add the egg yolks and sugar to the bowl and whisk constantly, slowly heating the mixture until the sugar dissolves and the egg yolks double in size and lighten in color, about 5 minutes. (The mixture should reach 100°F and be thick and pale yellow.) Set aside to cool completely.

4. Meanwhile, in a large bowl (or you can use a stand mixer for this), whisk the heavy cream until stiff peaks form.

5. Gently fold the whipped cream into the cooled egg yolk mixture. Add the honeydew juice and salt and fold, again gently, until just combined. Transfer this pale, green-tinted mixture to the loaf pan, cover with the overhanging plastic wrap, and freeze until firm, about 4 hours or overnight.

6. To serve, let the covered semifreddo sit out at room temperature to thaw for about 5 minutes before unmolding and slicing into thick slabs. Covered, this will keep for up to 2 weeks in the freezer.

Gochujang Chocolate Lava Cakes

The talented food writer, baker, and author of *Cookies*, Jesse Szewczyk, suggested that I try combining gochujang and chocolate in one of my desserts. I was hesitant at first, but when I added a smidge of the fermented chile paste to my lava cakes, it transformed them completely—in a wonderful way. The salty, fermented notes of gochujang add great depth and savoriness to the gooey-sweet chocolate cake, leaving behind some heat on the tongue, which obviously feels paradisiacal for heatseekers like me. To add to the chile-spiked aroma of the dessert, I also suggest a light dusting of gochugaru powdered sugar.

There's no flour here because I adore the meringue-like chew of a flourless chocolate cake, and the fat is olive oil because the fruitiness and ease delight me. And remember the no-churn vanilla bean ice cream on page 261? That soft coolness would be excellent against this hot, chocolatey moltenness.

Cooking spray

4 ounces bittersweet chocolate (60% or more cacao)

¼ cup plus 2 tablespoons olive oil

2 large eggs

½ cup granulated sugar

1 teaspoon vanilla extract

1 teaspoon gochujang

Pinch of kosher salt

Powdered sugar, for garnish (optional)

Gochugaru (optional), for garnish

Vanilla ice cream, store-bought or homemade (page 261), for serving

MAKES 4 SERVINGS

1. Preheat the oven to 400°F. Mist four 6-ounce ramekins with cooking spray and place them on a sheet pan.

2. In a small microwave-safe bowl, melt the chocolate in the microwave in 30-second intervals, checking and stirring between each zap, 1 to 2 minutes total. Set aside to cool slightly.

3. In a separate bowl, whisk together the olive oil, eggs, granulated sugar, vanilla, gochujang, and salt until light and fluffy, about 1 full minute. Gently stir in the melted and slightly cooled chocolate.

4. Pour the chocolate batter into the ramekins and bake until the tops have set and even cracked slightly (the insides will still be hot and gooey), 10 to 15 minutes. Use tongs and/or a kitchen towel to carefully transfer the hot ramekins to individual small plates (serve these immediately).

5. If desired, add equal parts powdered sugar and gochugaru to a sieve and gently dust the tops of the chocolate cakes. Serve a scoop of vanilla ice cream atop each ramekin.

Chewy Black Sesame Rice Cake

This simple yet regal cake tastes like a mix between songpyeon, that honeyed sesame-filled tteok served during Chuseok (the fall harvest festival), and those chewy black sesame rolls you might find at a Korean bakery. The best part is you only need a whisk and a bowl to make it. I love the way the cake batter's density forces the celestial black sesame crumble upward to form a perfect black line. This black line acts as a sweet, nutty brittle atop the squidgy vanilla base. The chewiness of this cake comes primarily from glutinous rice flour, often labeled as mochiko or sweet rice flour. You can get it online and at most grocery stores these days. But another key trick to chewiness in desserts, I find, is really whipping the eggs—a solid 1 to 2 minutes—to dissolve some of the sugar (like you would with French macarons) and to incorporate air, which causes baked goods like this one to rise and deflate as it cools, adding to that wonderful chewy texture. It helps, too, that this is the easiest, most straightforward cake recipe I've ever developed.

Cooking spray

2 large eggs

1 cup sugar, plus more for sprinkling on top

¼ cup honey

¾ teaspoon kosher salt

1 cup whole milk

1 tablespoon vanilla extract

2 tablespoons unsalted butter, melted

½ teaspoon toasted sesame oil

4 tablespoons toasted black sesame seeds

1 teaspoon baking powder

8 ounces (227 grams) glutinous rice flour (aka mochiko or sweet rice flour)

Powdered sugar, for serving

MAKES ONE 8-INCH CAKE

1. Preheat the oven to 350°F. Mist an 8-inch round cake pan with cooking spray.

2. In a large bowl, whisk together the eggs, sugar, honey, and salt until fluffy and pale yellow, 1 to 2 minutes. Whisk in the milk, vanilla, melted butter, and sesame oil until combined.

3. Using a mortar and pestle (or a coffee/spice grinder), pulverize 2 tablespoons of the black sesame seeds into a rough powder. It should smell very fragrant. Add this sesame powder, along with the remaining 2 tablespoons of whole black sesame seeds, to the bowl with the egg mixture, followed by the baking powder and rice flour. Whisk to combine, then carefully pour the batter into the greased cake pan.

4. Bake until the top is nicely browned and cracked slightly (this is a good sign), 50 to 60 minutes. You can also insert a chopstick or toothpick into the center of the cake, and if it comes out clean, then you're done.

5. Cool completely before dusting with the powdered sugar and slicing into wedges to serve. This cake will keep in an airtight container at room temperature for up to 5 days.

Whipped Cream Snacking Cake
with Fresh Fruit

I thought about closing this book with one of those perfect Korean bakery-style fresh cream cakes, with the multiple layers, the impeccable frosting, and the fresh fruit glistening with apricot jam. But deep down I knew that I would never actually make one of those myself. What I do enjoy baking at home are snacking cakes: single-layer sponges that don't require any frosting or layering skills. But because a snacking cake doesn't have the impressive layers of a store-bought Korean bakery cake, I needed to make sure this one was just as stunning—and just as delicious.

The cake itself is light and spongy, almost diaphanous, texturally reminiscent of those delicate cream cakes many Korean Americans grew up buying from Korean bakeries for loved one's birthdays. But its flavor is more American: robust, sugary, and full of the rich assertiveness of butter and vanilla. Still, as is a grand trait of Korean desserts, the pompadour of cool whipped cream and the glossy bed of macerated fruits (which ooze their tart-sweet juices into the cake) provide balance and measure to the otherwise buttery cake beneath. This recipe calls for strawberries, peaches, and kiwis, but you can use whatever you like. Mandarins, blueberries, and raspberries are also fair game.

This is a celebration cake, the one you should make when blowing out candles, commemorating an anniversary, or sending someone off. It's humble by nature, but still special enough for an occasion—or Thursday night. The ROI on this cake is very high, which is to say, for very little effort (you don't even need an electric mixer), you get a really good cake. It's the cake you should make when telling a boy you love him, or a friend that you appreciate them, or a mother that you are who you are because of her. It's a thank-you cake. This cake is special, to be sure, but it's also the cake you should make when you just want to eat cake.

Tip If you're not eating the cake for a while, be sure to store it in the refrigerator, covered, for up to 2 days. After that, the fresh fruit will start to break down too much and the cream will weep. The price of whole foods.

FOR THE CAKE

Cooking spray

¾ cup whole milk

1 teaspoon rice vinegar

1 stick (½ cup) unsalted butter, at room temperature

1 cup sugar

½ teaspoon kosher salt

2 large eggs

1 tablespoon vanilla extract

1 teaspoon baking powder

1½ cups (168 grams) cake flour

FOR THE MACERATED FRUIT

½ pound strawberries, hulled and halved, plus 5 whole strawberries for garnish

1 peach, pitted and cut into fat wedges

2 kiwi, peeled and thinly sliced crosswise

1 tablespoon maple syrup

FOR THE WHIPPED CREAM

1 cup heavy cream

2 tablespoons sugar

1 teaspoon vanilla extract

Pinch of kosher salt

MAKES ONE 8-INCH CAKE

1. Make the cake: Preheat the oven to 350°F. Mist an 8-inch round cake pan with cooking spray and line the bottom with parchment paper.

2. In a liquid measuring cup, measure out the milk and splash in the vinegar. Set aside to curdle a little while you prepare the rest of the batter.

3. In a large bowl, using a wooden spoon, cream the butter, sugar, and salt until smooth and fluffy. Add the eggs and vanilla and switch to a whisk to incorporate air into the mixture and to dissolve the sugar crystals some, about 1 minute. Gently stir in the baking powder and half of the flour until just incorporated. Stir in the milk, then add the remaining flour and mix until just incorporated.

4. Pour the batter into the prepared cake pan and bake until a chopstick (or toothpick) inserted into the center of the cake comes out clean, 30 to 40 minutes. Set aside to cool on the counter.

5. Meanwhile, macerate the fruit: In a medium bowl, toss the halved strawberries, peaches, and kiwi with the maple syrup and set aside to macerate until you're ready to assemble the cake.

6. To assemble, invert the cake onto a large plate or cake stand and arrange the macerated fruits atop the cake so the entire surface is evenly covered. Spoon or pour the remaining juices (there will be some at the bottom of the bowl) over the fruit, letting the cake soak them up while you make the whipped cream frosting.

7. Make the whipped cream: In a large bowl (you can use a stand mixer for this), whisk together the heavy cream, sugar, vanilla, and salt until thick and spreadable. It should have the consistency of, well, whipped cream—a soft-set one. Pile the whipped cream over the fruit, covering them entirely and spreading the cream almost to the edges of the cake.

8. Garnish the cake with the reserved whole strawberries and serve immediately.

Epilogue

A month before the manuscript for this book was due, I drove up to the Blue Ridge Mountains in Georgia to hole up in an Airbnb with my dog, my laptop, and two notepads filled with the recipes my mother and I had developed together that year. The main goal: get some writing done. I had read that the *New Yorker* staff writer Jia Tolentino took monthly writing retreats upstate to get high, eat pasta, and finish her superb collection of essays, *Trick Mirror.*

My trip to the mountains was sort of like that. And what I mean to say is: It was nothing like that. There was a lot of reading and a lot of thinking and definitely pounds and pounds of pasta—but the writing eluded me. By the time the Airbnb host was pinging me about my checkout at the end of the week, I looked down and hadn't written a single word of my manuscript.

"Inspiration will come to you when you're not looking for it" was the general message I got from Mother Nature that week. This was a problem because I was looking for it. But I did find myself taking pleasure in the small things again, like hiking in the mountains with my dog, reading *Harry Potter* (the sixth one, my favorite), and standing over the sink eating pasta every night straight from the pot. I loved that stupid cabin because the version of myself that resided there was a seventeen-year-old boy again. I laughed at my face whenever I walked by a mirror. It looked funny. I had a little muffin top hanging over my waistline, not unlike Hank Hill's, and the shadowed twilight of a patchy, pubescent mustache.

That week, life was a time warp. It was my first time on my own in a while, after quarantining with my parents in Georgia for a year, and developing the recipes you are reading here in *Korean American.* The excitement I felt at being alone again reminded me of the first time I left home for college in New York, where I would live for the next decade—873 miles away from my home, my childhood, my mother. It made me realize something: No one ever tells you that adulthood happens in two stages.

The first stage is clunky, full of adventure, and ultimately rewarding despite all the challenges of growing up. I remember the day I moved out for college, watching my mother's face turn redder and redder in the rearview mirror as my dad backed out of the driveway and drove me to the airport. After I landed in New York, he called me to make sure I had made it safely to my dorm, and to tell me that when Jean walked into my empty bedroom later that day for the first time, she burst into tears.

The second stage of adulthood gets less press. This is the homecoming stage, when the protagonist returns home. Homer's *The Odyssey* is the most popular example of this: The "returning home" part, a literary theme called nostos (a root of the word nostalgia, by the way), is considered the greatest honor because it means you've survived all the challenges out in the real world—the Sirens, the one-eyed giants, and the six-headed monsters; the unforgiving boss, the disgusting starter apartment, the crushing relationship . . . In narratology (the study of narrative), the hero's journey starts with a departure and ends with a return, the implication being that the adventure has transformed the hero for the better. Coming home means you've triumphed over death, or worse: temptation. Coming home means you can finally rest.

Despite this seemingly positive narratological conceit in literature, it doesn't quite translate as nicely when you apply it to modern-day homecomings in the real world. That's because in the real world, the reasons for moving back home are usually more traumatic: Maybe you've lost your job or are getting a divorce. Maybe someone you love has just died, and there's no one else to take care of the family business. Or maybe there's a global pandemic and you've never thought so much, so deeply, about your parents' mortality and the preciousness of time. Maybe you're just homesick.

In Korean culture, and indeed in many immigrant households, children live with their parents until they get married. There is no in-between stage that prepares you for the freedom of living on one's own, because adulthood is meant to be new, traumatic, life-changing. There are exceptions to this rule, of course, but as I lived with my mother for the better part of this year to write my book, I realized what a gift it was to get to live like this again. To live like you're seventeen. Nestled in the past, in the comfort of my mother's ministration, I was able to chronicle our family's history—and everything on our dinner table—cradled in a gently rocking canoe of nostalgia.

The Czech writer Milan Kundera wrote that "nostalgia is the suffering caused by an unappeased yearning to return." I believe that we as people reside, dwell, and relish in the first stage of adulthood for far too long and never fully make it to the second stage. Caught up in the hustle and bustle of our daily lives, we don't recognize the pain we're causing ourselves by not "returning." So many of us don't get to complete that hero's journey. Maybe we're too proud to move back in with our parents, or, something that's very common: Maybe the childhood home doesn't even exist anymore, physically. When homecoming is no longer an option, the hero must complete his journey elsewhere. Sometimes the journey isn't just leaving and returning home, it's figuring out where home even is.

That's my point about this second stage of adulthood: There's great bravery in the choice not just to return home, but also to *call* something home. For those of us who have felt uprooted as children of immigrants, in between nationalities, deciding to call a place home is part of the journey. Is it Korea or is it the United States? I'll never take for granted the courage it took my parents to immigrate here and to start a new life from scratch—to decide to call this strange, open space "home." And some of us spend our whole lives searching for it, trying to define it. Luckily, if there's any doubt, one reliable way to find home is to go where family is. There's a reason why holidays like Thanksgiving and Christmas can feel so restorative. We need family. Family heals. Whether that family is biological, adopted, or found, everyone deserves a slice of it.

If there's one thing I've learned from my year of writing this book, it's how much more whole we are as humans when we carry our families with us wherever we go. It's half a life trying to do everything alone all the time. We are who we are because of where we come from, and one way to find ourselves when we're especially lost is to return to our place of origin, if only for a bit. Not to mention that returning home, or revisiting the past, is one way to better understand the present. I'm forever grateful to this book because it brought my family and me together again in ways that I could never have anticipated. It was, first and foremost, a year of translation. I used to resent my role as my parents' translator, from signing my own permission slips in grade school to helping them vote for the first time as American citizens. But as I get older, I'm starting to recognize this role as an incredible privilege, an honor, and, frankly, the least I could do.

This book isn't just about Jean, or my family, or Korean American home cooking. It's a love letter to Atlanta, as well. A place, a feeling, a

> We are who we are because of where we come from, and one way to find ourselves when we're especially lost is to return to our place of origin, if only for a bit.

time period. I used to think I hated Atlanta. But I've realized something: This tension many of us feel with our respective hometowns might come less from our hatred for the actual cities and more from a desire to move on from the incomplete versions of ourselves who used to live there. That's why leaving home is only the first stage of adulthood. It's the second stage where you really, as they say, grow up. At least in my experience. It takes going back home to recognize that the whole story is as important as the ending. The more I wrote about Atlanta and its mountains, its lakes where you can go fishing, all those deciduous trees lining the highways, roads, and streets that are named after peaches, the more I dreaded leaving it behind again.

When I was in that Airbnb trying to write this book alone, I felt paralyzed. I couldn't do it. Everything was too still; I missed the constant bustle of a packed house. This surprised me because prior to this, I had been living alone in New York City for more than ten years. I even wrote a weekly column about it. So what was this newfound loneliness I felt in some random wood in the mountains of North Georgia? This debilitating solitude? Luckily, they all drove up to visit me and my dog for a couple days: my mom, dad, brother, and Ladie, the Shiba Inu. It reminded me of that busy, awkward energy when parents visit their kid at college for the first time: The parents want to respect the kid's newfound independence; the kid is eager to show the parents the new "adult" version of themselves, which at this point in life is probably only a stone's throw away from playing house. But for me, as a grown man with a newly adopted beer belly, when I found out that my parents were visiting me in the mountains, I was overjoyed because it meant one thing: They could bring me cake.

I had packed tomato paste and pasta and instant ramyun and all manner of wines and sodas, even my heaviest food encyclopedias. But I hadn't thought to pack a single candy bar. I had forgotten one of life's greatest pleasures, dessert. In the discomfort of that stranger's Airbnb cabin, I realized how much I needed the comfort of a simple slice of cake. I texted Jean that I was craving something sweet ("but not too sweet"), so she stopped by a Korean bakery on the way up and brought me a cream cake—like, a whole one—one of those perfectly layered vanilla sponges with whipped cream as frosting and a kaleidoscope of fruits nestled within. You've seen it before; there's an emoji for it.

When my family arrived at the cabin with the cake, they told me they were glad I went away for the week because it meant that they could

The more I wrote about Atlanta and its mountains, its lakes where you can go fishing, all those deciduous trees lining the highways, roads, and streets that are named after peaches, the more I dreaded leaving it behind again.

start eating "healthy" again (whatever that means). I guess I saw their point. At one juncture in the book-writing process, while working on the dessert chapter, I was baking a fresh loaf of milk bread every morning—and every day, my family ate the whole thing. They blamed me for their gluttony, even though they should've blamed the milk bread for being so delicious. Funny thing is, this book almost didn't have a dessert chapter because, as was my false explanation at the time, "Koreans don't eat dessert." Which is obviously not true. But in our house, after dinner, dessert was never really a slice of cake or pie or a tray of cookies. It was always a plate of peeled, sliced fruit: apples, for sure, and Korean pears, which are crisp and refreshing, and chamae, an oblong yellow melon with crunchy, honeyed seeds within. Maybe strawberries, peaches, kiwi . . . When I think of that iconic cream cake, brimming with fresh fruit, I can't help but feel that it's so much more than just a birthday cake. It's a symbol of one community's shared nostalgia, and their ultimate sense of belonging.

When I first arrived in Atlanta to be with my parents, it was late July, my twenty-ninth birthday. I'll be thirty when this book comes out, but I feel seventeen again. On one of my last nights in Atlanta, as I was walking

my dog, Q, through this sleepy suburb where I've lived my whole life, I smelled my mother's makeup because I had grabbed the wrong face mask again. Even though I've done it a thousand times before, I kept thinking how sad it's going to be, this time especially, to drive away from this house, from my childhood, and from my family, waving good-bye to Jean as she stands in the driveway turning red again. Drive safely. See you at Thanksgiving, Christmas, New Year's. Kakao me when you get there. I love you more than you know. I can't live without you. You've changed my life. Thank you for everything.

Acknowledgments

As with everything else in my life, the story of this book starts with Jean, to whom I owe everything. I am who I am because of you, Mom, and it's been the greatest honor of my life getting to know you better this year, not just as a mother, a daughter, a sister, and a cook, but also as a person.

Thank you to my family—Dad, Kevin, Juhee, Becky, and all the aunts, uncles, and cousins—for testing and tasting recipes, helping me with dishes, and running out for groceries whenever I was juggling Zoom calls and book deadlines, and, ironically, forgetting to eat meals. I could not have done this without you.

I am especially indebted to the talented folks at Clarkson Potter who worked so hard on this book. First and foremost, a weighted blanket of gratitude to Raquel Pelzel, who believed in this project, and in me, from the start. I've never missed so many deadlines in my life, and I'm grateful to have had someone with your empathy to guide me through my first book. Thank you, as well, to Bianca Cruz for keeping us on track, to Marysarah Quinn for designing with such grace, to Francis Lam for the encouragement, to Aaron Wehner for giving *Korean American* a home, and to Erica Gelbard, Windy Dorresteyn, Stephanie Davis, Kate Tyler, and Allison Renzulli for cheering me on from the beginning.

A huge thanks to my agent, Katherine Cowles, without whom my career as it stands would not exist. Your mentorship—but most of all, your friendship—has changed my life in the most fulfilling ways. I'm so lucky to have met you.

Thank you to my incredible photographer, Jenny Huang, who led and built out the visual storytelling of this book with unparalleled artistry; to my prop stylist, Beatrice Chastka, who captured the spatial and temporal essence of *Korean American* with great care and attention; and to my food stylist, Tyna Hoang, who expertly cooked the recipes in this book with emotional intelligence and always with the main narrative in mind:

food that tastes like home. Thanks, as well, to Pierce H. Liu, Scotty Fletcher, and Charlotte Havelange.

To my recipe testers, Kat Craddock and Rebecca Firkser: I can't believe I know such talented cooks and editors. Even more, I'm so honored to call you my friends.

Speaking of which, I would not have survived this grueling journey without my dear companions who were going through the same with their own books. I love you, Rick Martínez, Mayukh Sen, Jesse Szewczyk, and Yewande Komolafe.

I'd also like to thank Genevieve Ko, Emily Weinstein, Sam Sifton, and everyone at *The New York Times* Food desk who inspire me and make me a better writer, reporter, and recipe developer every day. I still can't believe I get to work with such talents.

Many thanks to Michelle Buffardi for plucking me from the gutters of academia, and to Irene Yoo for reading my manuscript in its early stages. Irene, this book would not have been the same without your expertise or your friendship.

And finally, thank you to Paolo, who reminds me every day that home is where the food is.

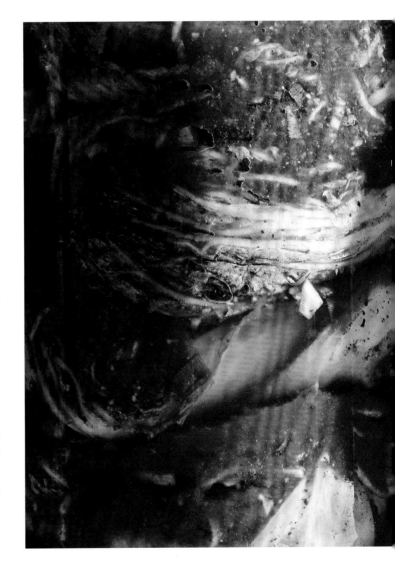

Index

Note: Page references in *italics* indicate photographs.

Published in the United States by
Clarkson Potter/Publishers, an imprint
of Random House, a division of
Penguin Random House LLC,
New York.
clarksonpotter.com

CLARKSON POTTER is a trademark
and POTTER with colophon is a
registered trademark of Penguin
Random House LLC.

Library of Congress
Cataloging-in-Publication Data
Names: Kim, Eric, author. | Huang,
    Jenny, photographer.
Title: Korean American: food that
    tastes like home.
Description: New York: Clarkson
    Potter/Publishers, 2022.
Identifiers: LCCN 2021031286 (print)
    | LCCN 2021031287 (ebook) | ISBN
    9780593233498 (hardcover) | ISBN
    9780593233504 (ebook)
Subjects: LCSH: Cooking, Korean.
Classification: LCC TX724.5.K65 K5428
    2022 (print) | LCC TX724.5.K65
    (ebook) | DDC 641.59519—dc23
LC record: lccn.loc.gov/2021031286
LC ebook record: lccn.loc.
    gov/2021031287

ISBN 978-0-593-23349-8
Ebook ISBN: 978-0-593-23350-4

Printed in China

10 9 8 7 6 5 4 3 2 1

First Edition

Photographer: Jenny Huang
Food Stylist: Tyna Hoang
Prop Stylist: Beatrice Chastka
Designer: Marysarah Quinn
Editor: Raquel Pelzel
Editorial assistant: Bianca Cruz
Production editors: Katy Miller,
Mark McCauslin
Copy editor: Kate Slate
Production supervisor: Kelli Tokos
Compositor: Merri Ann Morrell
Indexer: Elizabeth T. Parson
Marketer: Stephanie Davis
Publicist: Erica Gelbard